No Bars Hold

No Bars Hold

John White

Library of Congress Control Number: 2010900682
ISBN: Hardcover   978-1-4500-3420-3
                 Softcover   978-1-4500-3419-7
                 E-book   978-1-4500-3421-0

John White
PO Box 1124
Toodyay 6566 Western Australia
+61895745403
Email: jandjwhite@westnet.com.au
www.magpieridgeproductions.com.au

This book was printed in the United States of America.

To order additional copies of this book, contact:
Xlibris Corporation
1-800-618-969
www.xlibris.com.au
Orders@Xlibris.com.au

500071

CONTENTS

Introduction...9

    I   No Bars Hold 17

   II   Prisoner 31

  III   Don't Look For the Living 40

  IV   Spirit and Fire...52

   V   As A Doe..66

  VI   Travel Far and Wide 79

 VII   Image of You (Song for Stephanie).........................92

VIII   I Was Hungry 103

  IX   How Full of Wonder..114

   X   Turn Around...126

  XI   The Sky's No Limit..137

Conclusion 153

Acknowledgements

For Jennifer, my wife and constant companion for 35 years, for Emma and Benjamin, our two wonderful children, for Alan and Kylie their spouses, and for Hamish and Nathan, our delightful grandsons. I am thankful that our lives are joined.

For my cousin and friend, Kim Stedman, without whose encouragement the CD, *No Bars Hold,* would never have been released, nor this book written. I would be the poorer for not having the experience of engaging in this way with the Spirit.

For my friend, Rev Dr Jeff Sturman, for his diligent reading of the early drafts and for helpful comments and constant friendship.

For the inexpressible mystery of God in whom I find myself continually finding myself.

Introduction

*T*wo crows thought they'd try something they hadn't tried before. They'd steal an egg from the eagle's nest. The plan was for one crow to distract the eagle while the other crow stole an egg and made off with it. They achieved the theft and flew down to the forest floor to eat their prize. But a disagreement erupted over who should have the larger share, and they began fighting. The egg was left on the ground while they chased one another, clawing, pecking and flapping through the forest.

A farmer who was walking in the forest near his home observed the entire event and came upon the egg lying on the grassy track. He bent down and picked it up. The egg was warm. Returning home some time later, he took off his coat and, remembering the egg, he took it out to his chicken pen and placed it secretively under one of his hens sitting on some of her own eggs.

After a time, one by one the chickens hatched; six fluffy yellow ones and one white one with brown speckles. They followed the hen around the yard pecking like she did at worms and insects and, eventually, grain given to them by the farmer. The yellow chickens changed their feathers for white ones, and grew to adulthood. The speckled one grew many times larger than the others and turned dark brown with white specks on his breast and white on the feathers at the tips of his huge wings. He had *a large, hooked beak, piercing eyes, long, strong, feathered legs, huge talons, and he flapped and pecked and clucked like all the others.*

One day a shadow moved across the yard and, looking up, he noticed a huge, majestic bird soaring effortlessly high above. 'Who is that'? he asked his mother in awe. 'That is the eagle' his mother replied; 'the king of the forest'. 'Why don't we fly with him' he asked his mother. 'She replied, 'we are chickens; chickens don't fly'. So the young eagle lived and died as a chicken. (Indian folklore)

This little book is a companion to the music CD of the same name. In essence, the songs parallel the tragedy of the eagle story. They are about finding and living our True Selves rather than the limited selves many of us live because we simply don't know who we really are; we haven't been encouraged to find out.

No Bars Hold is a partial expression of what is true for me. Because, as a human being, I am not static, but shift in awareness, understanding and expression with each new experience of my life, words written before today no longer accurately represent me. Where there is a departure to any significant degree, I will indicate in order to offer you what I believe to be the best I can at this moment in time.

The songs in this collection and the words written about them have come from my struggle over the years to engage with the depths of who I am as a being. They speak of an emerging inner knowing—or faith—that is stronger than intellectual knowledge. They speak of hope, which is stronger than despair. And they speak of my belief and experience that love is stronger than fear.

One of the challenges in writing anything, is that use of words is a potentially dangerous practice. Words mean different things to different people. They are, literally, loaded with the meanings and, often, powerful emotions that our life experiences and beliefs give to them. One person's use of the word 'joy', for example, may be to express a quiet, deep, inner security and contentment. Another person may use the same word for noisy, exuberant laughter and celebration.

This is a book about spirit, and it is spirit that gives us life. It is not easy to talk about spiritual matters without mentioning God. But the word 'God' is one of the most loaded words we have invented, because we each have our personal understanding and experience (or not) of this mystery that some of us call God.

So, in order to have the essence of this book understood in a way that I hope is helpful, I'll try to sketch at the outset what I mean by God. And I'll mention, here, a few other terms that are widely used to attempt to express this inexpressible mystery. I am aware that in doing so in the way I am about to, I may be asking some of us to jump in at the deep end. If the next passage seems like that, I hope you will just let it sit where it is and, perhaps, return to it after reading some of the material to follow. The truth is that this 'mystery' we are dealing with here *is* deep; it is beyond the capacity of the human mind to fathom. And we like to fathom things. Our training is to reason and understand. But although this mystery remains outside our understanding, it is sufficiently knowable in ways other than reasoning for us to engage with it. So, even though it may seem difficult, I am confident that as we consider the thoughts to come—which are all associated with the great mystery—the way will become comfortable enough for us to persevere.

What is this 'transcendent mystery', this 'ultimate truth', this 'universal Law'? These are words we use to express the inexpressible. This is the whole problem of life, which continually baffles our reason. The ultimate meaning and purpose of life cannot be expressed, cannot properly be thought. It is present everywhere, in everything, yet it always escapes our grasp. It is the "Ground" of all existence, that from which all things come, to which all things return, but which never appears. It is 'within' all things, 'above' all things, but it cannot be identified with anything. Without it nothing could exist, without it nothing can be known, yet it is itself unknown. It is that by which everything is known, yet which itself remains unknown It is 'unseen but seeing, unheard but hearing, unperceived but perceiving, unknown but knowing' (Brhadaranyaka Upanishad 111.8.11). This is the mystery upon which both Indian and Chinese thought lighted in the sixth century before Christ. They called it Brahman, Atman, Nirvana, Tao, but these are only names for what cannot be named. We speak of 'God', but this also is only a name for this inexpressible Mystery.

This mystery lies behind all religion, from the most powerful to the most primitive. Thus it is said of the American Indians: 'The Tlingit do not divide the universe arbitrarily into so many different quarters ruled by so many supernatural beings. On the contrary, supernatural power impresses them as a vast immensity, one in kind and impersonal, inscrutable as to its nature, but whenever manifesting itself to men, taking a personal, and it might be said, a human personal form in whatever aspect it displays itself. Thus the sky spirit is the ocean of supernatural energy that manifests itself in the sky, the sea spirit as it manifests itself in the sea, the bear spirit as it manifests itself in the bear, the rock spirit as it manifests itself in the rock . . . For this reason there is but one name for this supernatural power, Yok, a name which is affixed to any specific manifestation of it'

In the same way, the religious faith of the Dakota . . . is in a mysterious and intangible something of which they are only the embodiment . . . the great object of all their worship . . . is the Taku Wakan, which is the supernatural and mysterious. No one term can express the full meaning of the Dakota's Wakan. It comprehends all mystery, secret power and divinity' (Bede Griffiths, Return to the Centre, Fount, 1978)

This, which is true of the American Indians and seems to be the basic pattern of all primitive religion, is also true of Hinduism. All the Gods (and Goddesses) are but manifestations of the one, infinite, eternal Brahman . . . the 'One' without a second, the unutterable mystery . . .

This inexpressible mystery is also variously termed Ground of being, Wisdom, Universal Truth / Law / Principle, Great Reality, Father, Allah, Brahman, Atman and a host of others. For what I hope will be clarity—as much as we can be clear about the unclear—I have tried to restrict myself to the single term 'God'; the term with which we in the west are most familiar, notwithstanding our plethora of individual understandings of what that term means for us.

What most people seem to agree upon in general terms, is that humankind is spirit by nature and manifesting in a material form in this life on earth. That's where our agreement usually ends. But that doesn't matter. None of us can say with certainly 'this is the truth'. So we need to exercise intelligence and humility to try to embrace this inexpressible mystery within ourselves, in each other and in the world in ways that contribute to life rather than diminishing, dividing and destroying life.

Two other terms that appear throughout the book need explaining here. These refer to what can be thought of as the 'two selves' in each of us, a reality accepted by most wisdom traditions. These two selves are often considered in terms such as lower or higher self, surface or deep self, outer or inner self, flesh or spirit, and a host of others. In many mystical traditions that marry depth psychology with depth spirituality, the terms often used for these two selves are 'ego' and True Self'. Throughout this book, these are the terms I will use.

Let me say something about the aspects of the human being to which each term refers. Because this is not the place for a comprehensive discussion about the psychological complexities of human beings, for simplicity and the purposes of this book we can think about ego in this way. It is that part of us that comprises our thinking, feeling and acting functions. The ego contains our beliefs, values, ethics and morality. It seems to be influenced by genetic predisposition, and evolves in reaction and response to every experience of life from the first breath to this present moment. The ego includes all the elements that make up personality, and is the part of us that interacts with the external world. It is essential for human functioning, and is the part of us that sets and maintains boundaries of all sorts to keep us safe and 'appropriate' in our day to day interactions with others and with the physical world. But because the ego's sphere is the transient world of material space and time, it is aware of the underlying fear of death and non-being—the great existential fear of the soul.

The True Self really can't be explained. The following statement by William Law provides a direction for us.

'For, though God be everywhere present, yet he is only present to thee in the deepest and most central part of thy soul. Thy natural senses cannot possess God or unite thee to him; nay, thy inward faculties of understanding, will and memory, can only reach after God, but cannot be the place of his habitation in thee. But there is a root or depth in thee from whence all these faculties come forth, as lines from a centre or as branches from the body of a tree. This depth is called the Fund or Bottom of the soul. This depth is the unity, the eternity, I had almost said the infinity of thy soul; for it is so infinite that nothing can satisfy it or give it rest but the infinity of God'.

William Law

Thomas Aquinas says it like this:

'only when man realizes that he himself is an inscrutable mystery—that is, that his true being lies beyond thought or consciousness that he may have of himself—only then can he discover in the depths of his experience the inscrutable mystery of God. Man's unknowable being is of the same order as God's, for man comes from God and has been created in his image. His is the 'beyond all' of Being itself'

(Aquinas, Summa Theologica),

Throughout this book the term True Self is used to refer to this inscrutable mystery that is who we really are.

My hope is that this little book and these few songs will be of assistance to us as we acknowledge the great longing inside ourselves, and engage with the Great Mystery in which we are all inextricably caught up, and in which somehow all is well.

Because this book is a companion to the CD, *No Bars Hold,* it is presented as a series of stand-alone chapters. Each can be read in isolation as each relates to one song. And because all the songs are on a common theme, to do justice to each, I felt it necessary to cover the ground relevant to each chapter. This means that there will be some repetition throughout the book as a whole, but I have tried to keep this to a minimum so as not to annoy the reader. Generally, any repetition will only be of central themes which, I hope, may serve to reinforce that which is useful to us.

John White
Toodyay, January 2009

Chapter One

No Bars Hold

J enny and I had been in Planet Recording Studios night after night for some time. We'd already recorded several tracks for our first album with the multi-talented musician and sound engineer, James Hewgill. At that time we didn't have a title for the album, or even much idea about what we were producing. We just had a few songs that we'd sung around churches and prisons, and that seemed to be well received by those who heard them. And we were passionate about doing what we could to encourage people who had been hurt by life in one way or another. There was a general thought that we'd like to produce a recording that would both help others experience freedom from the burdens they carried, and also raise some much needed funds for Prison Fellowship's work with prisoners, their families and victims of crime.

While James was doing his magic with the eight tracks we'd just put down, I was having yet another strong black coffee and a cigarette (James was a heavy smoker and I was mostly an ex-smoker until I started that recording). It was about three o'clock in the morning. It always seems to be about three o'clock in the morning when you're in a recording studio! When the creative juices start to flow they seem to produce a life and energy that won't allow you to stop and sleep. Often we'd take a break and roar down to Hungry Jacks or Kentucky Fried at the end of North

Lake Road in James' Cordia Turbo. The first time I got into this tiny car, I spontaneously cackled like a schoolboy at the sheer acceleration of the thing! I was staggered that such small engine could produce such power. But I digress!

Thinking about prisons made me think about bars, and that led me to consider the things that 'bar' us from fully and freely enjoying life. As I took satisfaction in coffee and tobacco smoke, it occurred to me that, right here, were two things that were probably barring me from certain aspects of full life. And off I went into a reverie reflecting on my own freedoms and lack of them, and how good it would be if we could live life with 'no holds barred'.

As I have long been impressed by the wisdom in many of the mystical religious expressions, I have come to love and value the 'circular' way of these traditions rather than the 'linear' way of the Western world. Things like Confucius' words, *'the one who speaks doesn't know; the one who knows doesn't speak'*. I love that! I love the challenge to become increasingly aware of what's going on in my mind, how wisdom is not unidirectional, and how that determines the openness and effectiveness of my living. So, as I'd always enjoyed playing with words anyway, and this circular way of processing life provided great encouragement for that, *'no holds barred'* simply became *'no bars hold'*. I knew in that moment that we had a title for the album. We just needed a title track and, by around four a.m., I had most of the song on paper and the tune in my head.

I believe it's true to say that we cannot *not* tell our own story; every experience of life becomes part of who we are at any given moment in time. What we think and believe informs what we say and do, and what we don't say and don't do. Nothing can be hidden or erased. It's all there in some form, and cannot help but be seen by aware observers, the group which, hopefully, includes us! In the past, scientists have talked about the scientific observer being objective. Now, most are realizing there's no such animal. Because the observer is there, any observations made are made through her or his subjective filters to at least some degree. Students of human interaction and communication tell us that most of what we say is said by our physical bodies and the tone of our voices. 'Your body is speaking so loudly that I can't hear your words'. An artist, an author, a critic, a gardener, an architect, a preacher, a parent, someone working, choosing a holiday, interacting with a human being, an animal or some other aspect of nature—whatever we do or observe being done, we are telling and seeing stories. So, when I write a song, I tell part of my story. I tell of my desire, my pain, my joy, my confusion, my passion. I speak of something that is significant about me and to me.

The song, *'No Bars Hold'*, is another part of my story. It's about my relationships, my work, my dreams, hopes, failures, losses and possibilities and much of what is me. That it seems to speak to many souls who hear it indicates that it is also part of the universal story.

Your prison may be the work you do, or the person who lives with you
Your prison may be the words you speak or the words you listen to
It may be the money that you have, or the money that you long for
It may be the pain you feel that no-one understands

Your prison may be the empty faces you see all around you
It may be the fear of letting someone see you as you are
It may be a door that's closed or a dream that now is broken
It may be of guilt and shame that years won't leave behind

(Refrain)
But no bars hold the smile that's born behind your eyes
No bars hold the hand of a friend who reaches out
No Bars hold the warmth in the heart that longs to touch another
No bars hold your spirit from rising to the Spirit of Life

Your prison may be a door that's closed or a dream that now is broken
It may be of guilt and shame that years won't leave behind
It may be a lonely cell and a price that you are paying
But you can be free right where you are in the life that bars can't hold

No bars hold, no bars hold, no bars hold your spirit from rising
To the Spirit of Life

Copyright: John White, August 1986

I am an idealist. In the depths of my soul, I have a kind of 'knowing' about how life could be. When I was younger, I used to say how life 'should' be. But I now understand that was just my idea and not necessarily 'the' way a person is to live. Through about 25 years of working as a psychotherapist, I have been privileged to meet thousands of people, most of whom had a dream for life too that was not being realized. And this is Australia, possibly the greatest country in the world in which to live at the present time. In this country, I have always been able to choose my preferred occupation. This is an incredible benefit not available to millions of my brothers and sisters throughout this world. My inner idealist caused me to be restless when I was younger, and I changed jobs every few years. Fortunately for me and my young family, meaningful work was available for the person I was. My idealist caused me to chose work in the helping professions of education, youth work, counselling and psychotherapy. And, although I have made many changes over the years, I have stayed in the same general field of helping others.

'*Your prison may be the work you do, or the person who lives with you*'. For me, my chosen profession provided enormous job satisfaction. I liked helping. In the early years, I was addicted to helping. I see now that I entered the profession largely for my own needs; I was a deeply insecure young man and needed the affirmation of others for me to feel good. I was a people pleaser for my first thirty five years. And it seemed to work at the time. I was nice to everyone, people liked me. One of the great benefits was that I developed great and diverse skill-set. It was a double-edged sword, really. I was both naturally adept physically and intellectually and had a passion for new experiences—particularly of the unusual and/or dangerous kind, and I needed people to be impressed with me. So becoming good at water skiing, getting a private pilot's licence, being able to run a farm on my own, building sheds and houses on my own, teaching myself enough guitar so I could accompany myself and Jenny professionally, becoming a nightclub singer, radio disc-jockey, abseiler, cruising yacht sailor and navigator, recording artist, high-school teacher, psychotherapist, etc, etc, satisfied both the need to express my natural inclination and restlessness, and to impress people and be helpful! My prison was in my need for all these things. If I had my time again, I'd do even more. The only thing I'd change (which young men and women don't have the awareness to change) is the motivation to impress others. I'd do everything only to enjoy it and I'd be in the moment rather than in the payoff.

It all looked pretty good. I thought I was successful. My wife and children weren't helped as much as other people, of course. That's part of the deal with pleasers. But I was so unaware, I felt hurt when I was criticized for 'never being home'. Couldn't they see? This was the price of being a helpful person and a good Christian man! Fortunately for me, my wife, Jenny, had great strength and perseverance and, probably, fear of living without me, and she stayed until I grew up enough to at least begin realizing what I was doing and why, and that it really wasn't so wonderful. I was driven to work; a workaholic. And even though I enjoyed it for it's own sake, the pain was in the lack of acceptance of my 'serving'. There was also pain in the reality that not everyone who was 'helped', either wanted help or used the help and changed their lives for the better! How ungrateful they were! These days I still carry the inner ideal, but am sufficiently aware to no longer be attached to it. So, if things work out, great! If things don't work out, great!

I was extremely fortunate. Many people hate their work. For them it is a prison.

At the time I wrote *'No Bars Hold'* I had just resigned from the Education Department where I'd been on permanent staff and working as a Personal Development Lecturer and Group Facilitator. In hindsight, this was an unwise move. I could have taken leave without pay and tested the new venture before jumping in. But I wasn't wise enough to do that or to listen to those around me who suggested less dramatic ways of making transitions. Such was my arrogance that I frequently cut off my nose to spite my face. This change meant a significant salary cut to start a counselling service for a youth welfare organization. It was a good thing to do and an ego trip! It's a shame they often come together! I have since found, that it is possible to be aware of both agendas, and to choose to avoid the demons in one of them! This particular job was to be short lived. Within two years I was made redundant. In my idealism, I challenged the boss for driving a luxury car and for some of the 'slick corporate' aspects of things that were said and done and, it seems, he didn't approve of that! One of my prisons was *the words you speak or the words you listen to'*.

Because you're reading this, you are a member of the human family. With membership of this family comes a range of experiences. Some of these are naturally pleasant; others are immensely painful. Existential psychologists tell us that anxiety, concern for meaning and purpose, and reflection on death and non-being are a few of the key 'sufferings' that come with the territory of simply being human. So, even though every human being experiences similar pain over similar issues, a common experience is also that there's *'pain you feel that no-one understands'*. It seems crazy and it's a deep tragedy, but a great many people spend much, if not all, of their lives at some level feeling alone and that no-one understands. Until I was about forty years of age, that was my experience. I played all the games, and anyone looking on would have no idea that I was feeling that, but I was. And we had been in a fellowship group of wonderful young Christians all raising our families and trying to do the best we could to follow the life and teachings of Jesus. But it didn't give us the power we needed, because we were young, thought we knew it all, had it all down pat in our heads, but the truth of the Spirit in God and man hadn't settled deep enough in any of us. Even in the midst of real and wonderful human warmth there can be a sense of a prison of *'the empty faces you see all around you'*. This phenomenon seems to be a thing of age. We start in the senses when we are infants, move to the mind as we develop our abilities, then to reason as our faculties become more sophisticated. But too few of us move beyond reason to 'Truth' that can only be found in stillness and silence within the human soul as it sees the unseeable and responds by surrendering; by letting go of doing and knowing and controlling, and is content to rest in being with what is.

Your prison may be the empty faces you see all around you
It may be the fear of letting someone see you as you are

It may be a door that's closed or a dream that now is broken
It may be of guilt and shame that years won't leave behind.

Why is it that faces around us can look empty? Is it that we see in them the lostness, the abandonment, that we experience within ourselves? Is it because we see in some faces a joy of life that we haven't yet found in ourselves and can't bear to face that painful reality? Is it because we don't recognize our own True Face that we are unable to recognize the True face of a brother or sister human being? I recall the words of a wise man by the name of Augustine who is reported to have said *'man has no rest until he finds his rest in God'*. Further he said, *'you do not find God because you seek without that which lies within'*. Without labouring the point, according to so many wise men and women such as Augustine, we fail to find our True Selves—our God selves, if you like—because we are constantly looking to others, to achievements, to money, to fame, to health, to anything else in creation for satisfaction of the inner longing to know our worth, our purpose and our meaning. When I find my face within my Self I will immediately see every other face as full of meaning and worth. I will know I belong to this great family. Most of us have tried everything we know; everything within our own strength and capability to make some sense of life and our part in it. But because life is so much bigger than us, we don't find it. It's a great paradox that only in a seed falling to the ground and dying, can it bear its fruit. In us choosing to allow our cleverness—our ego—to die, metaphorically speaking, we are enabling the great force of Life within us to rise and be amazingly present in all its glory, fullness and beauty.

Why is it that we are afraid of people seeing us as we are? Is it that we feel inferior and unworthy? Certainly many of the things we think and say and do in this life are such that we feel shame and guilt from time to time. And that's a good thing. The feelings are given to us as feedback on what is supportive of life and what is destructive of it. Our awareness of this feedback sets us apart from other creatures at least in this fact. We are able to reflect on ourselves, make choices, and accept or reject responsibility for those choices. A bit later we'll talk more about this. The truth about us is referred to in scriptures in many places. One such place is in the letter to the Roman Christian Church, chapter 8 verse 37 where it says, *'there is nothing in all of creation that can separate us from the Love of God in Christ Jesus'*. Much Scripture speaks of us being created in the image of God who is Love. Our challenge is to accept that we have no real power to create anything worthwhile in our own strength, that we are practically helpless and totally dependent on the Great Other who made us all and gave us everything we have, and that we are part of all that is. This acceptance opens a door to the life for which we are all longing and for lack of which we are suffering and dying alone. Willingly resting in the inner knowing that we belong to and in this great stream of life that we may call God, is the only way to experience the life we seek. Generally, the one place to which the stream runs is the ocean; the ocean of it's origin and destination. The sun evapourates water from the ocean, causing the vapour to rise and condense as clouds, which are driven by winds to high ground where they fall as rain and become streams that return to the ocean. In the same way, we come from and return to God. There is no escaping, no alternative route, nowhere we can go that allows life to continue to be refreshed. There are circumstances in which a stream is caused to take another route and is blocked by a sand bar or some other obstruction. It ceases to move, dries up or stagnates and dies as a stinking puddle. So, too, with us.

Doors close and dreams get broken and we feel pain. It is normal and essential for humans to dream. Scriptures say *'the people perish for lack of a vision'*. It's worth noting that the Hebrew word for 'vision' and 'dream' is the same word. We must dream. We must develop and maintain a vision beyond ourselves in order to cooperate with life taking us onward in a constantly renewing creative process. Our problems occur when we own the vision without reference to God; when we are attached to it. When we hold things tightly and a force comes upon them, they break. When we allow them to flow, the force shifts them but leaves them unbroken and somehow completed. Wisdom teaches us to hold our dreams courageously and, at the same time, lightly. As sun and rain come and go and we have no power over them, so we have no final power over the outcome of our dreams. But we certainly have significant control over the effort and commitment we bring to them. The importance of the dream is that it causes us to commence a journey, it calls us to choose directions, and it sustains us through all that we experience along the way.

And it is the journey that must be our focus, because we have this breath and this step, but not necessarily the next. That belongs to the giver of Life. Our responsibility is to accept with deep gratitude, and celebrate each gift as it comes. Then we are in the stream and flowing with all that is, rather than resisting. Then we are generous and filled with a deep care for all things, for we recognize ourselves as one of those things. Then we know there is no human worth more and none worth less than any other.

It has taken me more than fifty years to get anywhere near that way of knowing and being. Now, at sixty, although I experience a reasonable degree of contentment and security, I also know that I only glimpse the wonder and fullness of this mysterious thing called human existence. But I glimpse enough to be OK with that. I read in wisdom literature about being flowing and free, and not unhealthily attached to anything. And I experience moments of that free flow in times of silence and stillness, and in encounters with people and other parts of the glorious created order. I have been blessed with enough knowing not to be so anxious anymore. That's a relief. That feels good.

But no bars hold the smile that's born behind your eyes
No bars hold the hand of a friend who reaches out

No bars hold the warmth in the heart that longs to touch another
No bars hold your spirit from rising to the Spirit of Life.

Why do so few people smile at each other? Check out any elevator, footpath, shopping mall, etc, and see what I'm talking about. Maybe we're sad? Maybe we're afraid? Perhaps these two go together?

If we are created in the image of Love, how come we feel so much sadness or fear? And just in case you're not sure that we're created in, by and for love, why is love the experience everyone dreams of, desires, seeks, and feels most at peace with when even a glimpse arrives? We are made for it and by it and in it!

Our body's natural state is peace and joy. That's smiling inside and out! Smiling uses less muscles, less energy, produces more endorphins and other good stuff than frowning and other results of distress. And smiling is generated by love. A sunset, a tiny infant, rain when it's needed, a warm sunny spot on a cold morning, dew on a spider's web, a dramatic view of nature, the sight of a good friend or loved one all generate an inner and outer smile and bring the human into harmony. I recall recently I took my two year old grandson, Hamish, down to the river and we sat at the river's edge and threw pebbles into the water, watching the sunlight dancing on the splashes and ripples they made. For almost an hour we did that with variation and, at one stage, Hamish sat perfectly still, pebbles in each hand, a soft, semi-smile on his face, and an intently present yet far away expression in his eyes. The sunlight on rippling water, the gentle sound of the stream scrambling over rocks, a soft breeze soughing through the young sheoaks on the river bank, the dampness of the sand under our backsides, and the grit from pebbles in our hands. He was transfixed and transported; pure being, pure peace, pure joy for about two minutes. And I was transported by the experience of seeing him in that state of bliss! Then he continued throwing pebbles for a little longer before it was time to go home and do other things.

Love generates smiling and softness and joy. Fear generates scowling and tension and sadness. Because our true nature is love, there is a smile behind our eyes always. Our choice is to acknowledge its presence and give it space to be light and life to us and all who see it. And it's our choice to allow fear and the accompanying sadness to control us and unwittingly disallow the smile from bringing life to us and to the world.

This same inner spirit that moves our faces into light, moves our hearts and hands to reach out to any other to lift, guide, supply, celebrate their and our being family. The natural state for our hands is to reach out in friendship. When doing that our hands are exquisite. When doing violence they are ugly.

The natural state for the human soul or heart is to beat in unison with all other human hearts; to recognize itself in another and leap for joy at each encounter. And it is to sing in harmony with all of creation. The human heart is not beautiful when it isolates itself in fear, when it is not warm and generous towards all other creatures, and when it participates in any kind of destruction. Nothing can hold back the smile, the hands or the heart without our permission and cooperation. Of course, there are many times in life in which we feel sad or afraid. These are normal experiences of being human. And it is appropriate to look sad when we feel sad; great pain and damage is done to ourselves and others when we pretend to be what we are not at any given moment. But it is crucial for our individual and communal lives, and for the survival of life as we know it on this planet home of ours, to choose life and actively become part of the solution to the problems we are creating here.

And nothing is able to *'hold your spirit from rising to the Spirit of life'*. What does that mean? We've talked about the great stream of life—just another name for God. Just attempts to describe the indescribable. Those who seek to deeply encounter existence tell us the Spirit of Life runs through every particle of the universe. *(He (God) upholds the universe with his word of power' (Hebrews 1:3)*. And we are some of those particles with the added faculty of self-awareness should we choose to allow and develop that divine quality. And, rather than thinking 'up' or 'above', the use of the word *'rising'* is better considered as 'being beyond the constraints of our bodies and conscious human understanding'.

In life, we can't help but make choices. For most of us those choices are made from a position of incomplete or inaccurate information. For many of us, our choices are made in the environment of abuse, neglect or some form of violation either past or present. When this happens, we often find ourselves in trouble with the laws and norms of society, and are judged and punished accordingly. The sad reality is that, even though it is arguable that because of our circumstances we really couldn't have made any other choice, as adults we are still responsible for these choices and their results.

Over decades I have worked with men and women guilty of the most horrendous offences against humanity. Most of them start out minimising their actions, failing to acknowledge their victims or even denying that anyone has been victimised by their actions. These behaviours are developed ego defences to prevent the psyche from disintegrating at being confronted with the unbearable shame of such actions. Many psychologists call these ego-defences 'normal', as they are evident across the population of humanity. But they are really normal only to abnormal humanity, ie, one who doesn't yet know who he/she really is—a being created for love. To admit culpability for such inhuman behaviours is so painful to the psyche that, for survival, it must be dismissed in some way. So we learn to blame, rationalise, justify, displace the responsibility on to some other person, event or circumstance, and a raft of other strategies—all of which are out of our consciousness at least to begin with. The problem with these ego-defences being out of our consciousness is that we feel terribly hurt when someone challenges us. "I am not justifying; how could you be so unkind to me! If such and such hadn't happened, I wouldn't have . . . ." The only way from this point of death to life is through awareness; bringing that which is unconscious into consciousness. Then we have some choices about how to deal with ourselves. The more horrendous our actions, the more need we have to be separated from them. To be confronted with the shameful reality of what we've done and who we've become, it is first necessary to access some additional resources to enable us to cope with the pain the ego feels when we admit the truth. This is where the Spirit of God is indispensable. There is no other power sufficient to support us through deep shame than this inner knowing that, in spite of all the horror we've been part of and have become, we are still loved and lovable. Only as we come to know this inner Reality, can we face who we really are and begin healing and living the way life intends for us.

. . . .

Chapter Two

Prisoner

Michael and I met in about 1976. We've shared fair bit of life together since then, are still close friends, and still work together in the restorative justice movement gathering momentum in our West Australian prisons at present. Our children grew up together and are still in contact as 'good-friends', and our wives are close friends today and have been all that time.

Around 1978, one of Michael's friends was convicted of a business fraud and sentenced to a prison term at a place called Barton's Mill. This facility was originally a timber town and mill and, later, when the accessible forest had all been cut—another sad story in our often—inglorious history as a nation—Barton's Mill was taken over and modified by the West Australian Prisons Department for use as a minimum security prison. Michael wanted to visit his friend and encourage him through his imprisonment, so the two of us started visiting weekly. We discovered that there wasn't much encouragement for the prisoners at that time so, with our inmate friend, we decided that we would take a guitar with us when we went and we'd sing and talk and share a coffee and some supper. After a few visits, the singing and noise of guys being guys attracted a few others prisoners. Soon we had quite a gathering happening. We started taking our wives with us—a very much appreciated inclusion in a male prison! Needless to say, the number of inmates swelled! We had great times together and all looked forward to our weekly visits.

Around the same time the Watergate situation arose inside the United States government, and Charles (Chuck) Colson went to prison. During his time there, he was obviously challenged by his new situation in life to do some serious soul searching. Chuck experienced a spiritual transformation. It was a dramatic change. He came to the belief that inner transformation was essential if a prisoner was to not only take positives from his prison time, but to understand and deal with the issues that sent him to prison in the first instance, and heal his life so the cycle of criminal behaviour could be broken. Chuck formed Prison Fellowship International—a non-denominational, Christian based support service to prisoners and their families.

A little later Prison Fellowship (PF) came to Australia. Many Christian folk with hearts of compassion and knowledge that prisoners were brothers and sisters in the truest sense and no less worthy of being loved and supported than any other person, began forming small teams and visiting our prisons on a regular (usually weekly) basis. It was decided that our initial team to Barton's Mill would be most effectively administered under the auspices of Prison Fellowship, and teams developed into other prisons.

On our teams I continued to take my guitar and lead whatever singing the guys wanted—which was usually country, ballads and gospel. During those years we wrote a lot of our own songs to support any particular theme we were following with the guys on their various journeys—and we on ours, for that matter. I always remember thinking that we received more from the guys than they from us. They assured us that the reverse was true. It was a happy arrangement!

On one of the early teams was an older lady called Renie. She was a delight! Faithful, loving, gentle, never judging anyone, always had a deep peace and joy about her. Her faith in God had filled her with everything good and she could feel into the lives of the guys she loved and visited. On one of our visits—to Fremantle Prison, I think—she gave me a poem she had written, and asked me if I could put it to music. Because the original text was freely expressed from Renie's heart, the meter didn't readily allow it to be used as a song. So, with her permission, I made a few minor changes and *'Prisoner'* is the result. All the ideas are Renie's; my contribution is the adjustment, the musical score and the recording. When I read these words for the first time, they struck, in me, both my personal desolation in being lost and lonely at various times, and my deep gratitude for the easing of that pain that came with my beginning experience of the inner Christ. I had tears. Sometimes when I sing it now, I have tears. I can't help it.

I hope that as you read, hear and feel these words, something similar may happen for you. I hope, too, that you are able to experience something of the weird pleasure that comes with the privilege of visiting those in prisons of one kind or another. I hope you visit someone who suffers, and that someone visits you when you are in need. That's what makes life bearable and beautiful. We don't have to be in a prison cell to be *'feeling lost and lonely'* from time to time.

Are you feeling lost and lonely as you lay in your dark cell
Do you feel rejected by the world and there's no-one you can tell
About the way your heart is aching and life doesn't mean a lot
There's only gloom and darkness, not even one bright spot

(refrain)
Do not despair dear brothers, open your eyes, your heart and see

There's someone ever near you and he longs to set you free
Do not despair dear brothers, open your eyes, your heart and see
There's someone ever near you, and he longs to set you free

Call to him, Lord Jesus, I need you in my life
He'll call you out of darkness into his glorious light
Don't you know you're precious to him, just call upon his name
He's waiting now to tell you, you can be born again.

Don't you know you're precious to him, just call upon his name
He's waiting now to tell you, you must be born again
Then no longer will you be lonely, as you stand in your bright cell
His light is all around you, have peace for all is well.

copyright: John White (1981) (words by Renie Nears and John White, music by John White)

For around thirty years, my day job has been as a psychotherapist. Everyone who talks with me is in a prison of some kind. And I had and have my own also. Over the same number of years—although with considerable breaks during that time—I have been visiting prisons as a team member with PF. From my time with these prisoners, both within and outside jails, it has become clear to me that feeling lost, lonely, rejected, and with desperate heart-ache, darkness and meaninglessness are merely some of the experiences that come with the territory of simply being human. What I found to be most valuable in my own times of need, was a mature person—usually a stranger or, at least, a friend who was sufficiently secure within themselves not to put any of their agenda on me—to take the time and really hear me. It sounds simple, but being really heard at the depths of our souls from the depth of the soul of another, is one of the greatest acts of love and service one human being can do for another.

Actually, I chose to train in psychotherapy because a wise, compassionate, skilful man by the name of Ian Mackie, really heard me. I was about thirty two years old, and it was the first time I had experienced being heard. It felt so amazing, so freeing and energizing, that I decided there and then to provide that experience for as many people as I could for the rest of my life. The hearing wasn't indulgent; it simply, and truly acknowledged and validated my deepest pain as absolutely real for me. And then, with great gentleness and skill, Ian engaged me in the process of beginning to self-reveal the life that was in me to live. Not someone else's idea of how my life 'should' be; but mine. It's the right—and requirement, really—for each of us to find and live the unique life within us whilst, at the same time, realizing that we are each integral parts of the community of humanity, which is the essential context for these unique lives to have their fullest meaning and expression.

In addition to the human presence of the visitor, and the value of that, Renie talked easily and passionately about the comforting and healing power available in the Spirit-presence of the Christ of history and of all time. For Renie, her personal relationship with Jesus was the only thing with which to be concerned. At the time, I would have expressed my encounter in similar ways. And although relationships and understandings change with time, and I now express my spiritual experience somewhat differently, the reality is in no way diminished. Rather, it is deeper and stronger—if more mysterious—than ever.

It seems to me the western style societies we have created in our world are characterized by increasing stress, distress and despair. The inner unrest caused in large part by the dominant external focus on material aspects of living, is growing at an exponential rate. Anti-social behaviours in individuals, corporations and governments are increasing and seem to be tolerated as the new norm. Certainly ethics and morality of just a couple of generations ago are almost undetectable. Not so long ago, if a political figure was found to have committed an act that was not appropriate for his position in public life, he would resign his office. Not so now. Open dishonesty, manipulation, and self serving have become the norm, and political and other public figures practising such behaviours are re-elected time and again by a public who are, seemingly, not too perturbed by these behaviours.

We know that mental illness has become an epidemic, especially in developed countries. Anti-depressant and anti-anxiety medications are being prescribed to an ever-increasing number of people who are struggling with life. And with all our wonderful developments in medical science and technology, the situation is actually deteriorating. How can this be? Why are the most diligent efforts and solutions not having the desired effect?

Perhaps we only need to consider the wisdom of the ages to discover an answer. Much wisdom literature, thought and practice in humanity agrees that that man is a spiritual being functioning in a physical body and environment. For him/her to be well, s/he needs to acknowledge this truth and commit to giving primary energy and focus to nourishing this spirit essence. Whilst the Aboriginal peoples of Australia may not have lived the perfect life—no-one does—they sustained life as a culture for 60,000 years and lived in harmony with their environment. They produced no significant waste and made only limited changes to the eco-systems. And the maladies mentioned above that beset us non-indigenous people, were almost completely unknown to them. In comparison, we non-indigenous (to Australia) peoples have been here less that 300 years and, in that time, have brought, close to the point of collapse, both the natural environment and our mental, emotional and spiritual being. And we had the arrogance to consider ourselves as sophisticated and our dark brothers and sisters as primitive. A culture able to sustain itself relatively unchanged for tens of thousands of years has to be highly intelligent, sufficiently aware, and adequately wise. Yet we, in our arrogance and in what ought to be experienced as deep shame, despised this and many cultures like it throughout the world. Our white, western ways and our preoccupation primarily with the material aspects of life are clearly not working; deeply flawed.

Indigenous cultures have generally had a far deeper connection with the earth, its systems, and the spirit-mystery behind its coming into being than subsequent, so-called 'enlightened and sophisticated' non-indigenous peoples who displaced them. Indigenous cultures have traditionally taught and practised being aware of what is both around them and within them. They are grounded in seeing with the heart; seeing truly.

In the song, '*Prisoner*', the hearer is begged to '*open your eyes; your heart and see; there's someone ever near you, and he longs to set you free*'. Scriptures of major religions are held to be inspired by God, however the various religious seekers and communicators saw and named God. They speak of '*waking up*', '*rising from the dead*' (both physically and metaphorically), '*having eyes to see*', being '*born again*', receiving '*new life*', being '*saved*' (from themselves) and '*set free*'. Each of us, if honest, will admit to being hungry for something of such experience—even if expressed in different terms; something deeper; some meaning or purpose for our life. Some say '*call to him, Lord Jesus; I need you in my life*', he'll call you out of darkness into his glorious light'. The cry of another heart in distress or despair might call "God, help me" as a great many self-confessed 'non-believers' do in times of great trouble. There seems to be an inner knowing far deeper and more powerful than our rational minds; a knowing that spontaneously calls from its True Self to its Origin in times of deep distress.

If the Christ of history somehow mysteriously embodied the fullness of the creative power of the universe that we are here calling God, that's the power of help, life, freedom and healing that is being invoked by the one who calls. The 'name of Jesus' is not like saying 'abracadabra'; that would be an obscenity and a stupidity. Yet there are probably millions for whom this calling is merely a serious if, perhaps, misguided exercise of the mind that really hasn't made the deep connection with the inner reality embodied in that name, Jesus. In fact, it's probably not theologically sound to say *'I need you in my life'*. I think it's more appropriate to acknowledge that without the inner presence of the mysterious author of life, we don't have a life into which to invite anyone, let alone the Giver Himself! Kahlil Gibran alludes to this in his book, *'The Prophet'* in which he says, *"and when you love, do not say "God is in my heart; rather say I am in the heart of God"*. In that sense, the One to whom we call is not only *'ever near'*, but is already within. We are simply acknowledging that Reality and surrendering our ego-selves to it thus becoming free from self-imposed prisons.

Finally in these lyrics—and of central importance—is the deep knowing that we are *'precious'*; we are creatures of significant and permanent personal worth. This worth is nothing to do with us. It doesn't rely on how clever, articulate, attractive, etc that we are. Nor is this worth diminished by us thinking and acting in destructive ways. It is a given. Scripture says *'if we say we have no sin, we deceive ourselves and the truth is not in us. But if we confess our sin, he is faithful and just and will forgive our sin and cleanse us from all unrighteousness' (1 John 1:8-9)*. It doesn't matter that we have done wrong. All of us do wrong. What matters is that we recognize the wrong, take action not to continue it, return to and rest in the gift of acceptability which is ours again and again—as often as we realize error and return.

Many of us spend much, if not all, of our lives concerned about how we compare to others, how we perform, what others think of us, how much we achieve, what those achievements are worth, etc. None of those things alter the reality that we have a value of one; noone is worth 1.1; noone is worth 0.9. The true 'enlightenment', the true being 'born again', the true 'waking up' is to know—as a woman and man know each other in committed love-making—the transcendent, beyond-the-mind experience of union; to know that we have been given a worth; a value. And it is equal to the value of any other person ever.

Part of this essential lesson is that we are also equally very ordinary. Humility is deeply knowing and contentedly resting in this seeming paradox. When we know this, perhaps we can say we have 'found Love' and, only then, are able to give Love. Until then, what we think of as love is probably desire, need, dependency of some kind; a shadowy projection of our yet unknown soul. This essential knowing for living life as was intended, only comes from within the divine. This authentic calling of Jesus to God is the opening of the heart to the Divine Reality of life; the dispelling of darkness from our 'cells' in whatever form they exist.

Chapter Three

Don't Look For the Living

Before sunrise, tear-stained eyes headed for the tomb
Mary Magdalena, cradled in her gloom
Who will roll the stone away, who will heal the pain
Her last farewell, noone can tell the hope that has been slain

The stone has gone, so has the one, she came lookin' for
She runs to Simon Peter, 'they've taken away the Lord'
Peter and John set off at a run, to where the body had lain
An empty grave, a hollow cave and hope is born again

Don't look for the living, in the place of the dead
And don't let your sorrow erase what he said
And don't be discouraged now the darkness has fled
Don't look for the living in the place of the dead

'Tell me lady why do you weep, and who are you lookin' for'
She turns towards the gardener, 'I'm lookin' for the Lord'
Just one word, she'd never heard, a melody so sweet
'Mary' was all he had to call, and she's kneelin' at his feet

The news has spread, 'he's back from the dead', but some say it can't be true
Disciples in confusion, they wait in an upper room
A voice says 'peace' discussions cease, every face turns white
He said 'do not fear, cause I'm really here and everything's alright'

Copyright: Garth Hewitt

For many thousands of years—we'll leave the detail to the 'devil'—man has lived in reasonable harmony with her/his environment. The earth's eco-systems provided what was needed to sustain life, and man's impact on these systems was negligible. Most early societies have established ways of living that embraced physical, intellectual, and emotional functions, and most had, within their specific culture, profound and unified beliefs in a spiritual realm of some description which informed their lives before all else. Although we are not suggesting that ancient cultures got it all right, it could be argued that, in deferring with great reverence and awe to the Spirit world which, for them, was the Great Reality, they were on the right track.

In just a few hundred years, modern and post-modern man has developed such sophisticated technological skill that he can manipulate aspects of his environment as only 'gods' could in the understanding of earlier man. Although there is great potential for good in our cleverness, there is, it seems, even greater potential for death and destruction. It could be argued that we are now *'looking for the living in the place of the dead'.* We are looking to our intellectual and material abilities for life and have all but eliminated considerations of the spiritual; the very realm that, for thousands of years, has been intuitively known to be our source, purpose and destiny.

As in the previous chapter, I'd like to consider this search from two points of view: one, the specific person of Jesus who was dead and then was alive again and, two, the apparent folly of what we modern people are looking to to provide us with life and answers to our deepest questions.

It seems obvious from the destruction we have wrought on our natural world that our western way of being human is severely out of touch with what is sustainable. In just a few hundred years we have so changed this delicate balance in the eco-systems of our planet, that we are on the brink of rendering life as we know it to be unable to continue. For several decades, the best minds in the world have been sounding warnings that, if we continue the destructive path we are on, the earth and us will suffer very grave consequences. The scientific record in the earth indicates there have been five or six extinction events during the earth's history. The next extinction event, now in progress, will be the first caused by creatures, in this case, us.

There are two challenges. The first is to acknowledge that we are the problem and we must dramatically reduce our profligate consumption and degradation of the earth. The second is to access enlightenment and motivation to be able to do the first. The second challenge is really the first: if we don't first 'wake up and see correctly', we will not have the awareness to produce commitment and other resources to effect the drastic changes that are essential to our survival. Einstein said 'a problem cannot be solved with the same consciousness that created it'. And even if, by some stroke of magic, we could arrange to sustain life on earth with no reference to the spiritual reality providing and supporting our very existence, we would be 'dead men walking'. Being merely functionally alive, we would still be unable to live in harmony and peace with one another and with ourselves. The foundation must be sound for the building to be sound. If we fail to put the first step first, all other steps that follow will be of no avail. Scripture says it this way: *"Unless the Lord builds the house, its builders labour in vain" (Bible: Psalm*

127:1 NIV) It is written in many scriptures in various ways, *'seek first the Kingdom of God, and all other things will be added to you (Bible: Matthew 6:33) 'Plunge into the heat of battle keeping your heart in the lotus heart of the Lord" (Upanishads)* Here is a great place to allow ourselves to be grasped by the angel's words to Mary Magdelene outside Jesus' tomb: *'why do you look for the living in the place of the dead'?* In fact, to not be grasped by this great truth is to remain in darkness and slip inexorably into the oblivion of our self-destruction; to remain part of the problem rather than part of the solution. While in this darkness we cannot experience the intended bliss of being fully alive, fully human. We cannot experience being fully loved, loving, aware, walking lightly, eternally.

If you haven't read these stories of the historic Jesus interacting with ordinary people, I encourage you to read them. If you have, read them again. Examine your life again. Surrender everything again and experience life in all its fullness. The word 'surrender' may bring up some fear for you if you have been hurt by someone older or stronger than yourself at some stage in life. I am certainly not suggesting that you accept mistreatment or abusive behaviour of any kind. If that has been your experience, it may be helpful to discuss this idea of surrender with someone you trust who has the skill to help you be clear about what is and is not being suggested here.

The story begins,

"before sunrise, tear-stained eyes headed for the tomb
Mary Magdalena, cradled in her gloom
Who will roll the stone away, who will heal the pain
Her last farewell noone can tell the hope that has been slain'

If you've lost someone precious to you or know of someone close to you who has, you'll know something of the pain and confusion of emotions and thoughts that accompany such loss. Mary's grief was no different from any other human tragedy—gut-tearing, heart-rending pain; sadness, anger, questions of 'why him'? It's unfair, unjust, inhuman. He was guilty of nothing. In fact, he was more just, more loving, more life-giving than any of those bringing false charges against him and delivering his final punishment. More than all that, Mary had been violently torn from the only man who had truly accepted and loved her for her own sake; the only man who didn't take something from her. In her culture, women were not permitted to learn from a Rabbi. But Jesus welcomed women to talk with him and travel with him, thereby demonstrating that a woman was of equal worth to any man and is to be treated as such. Mary's seeking had been rewarded in this man, Jesus, who met her as a brother and treated her like royalty.

And no sooner had he appeared in her life and brought her a mind-swimming flood or light and life and love, he had been taken from her. And she grieved not only her personal loss, but the immeasurably greater loss to the whole world of the new and wonderful life that Jesus promised all who would follow his way of being.

As she trudged to the tomb in that pre-dawn gloom, her inner darkness and despair was indescribably deeper and darker. All was lost. The bright hope that had flamed for her for the briefest of glorious days, lay dead in a cave behind a huge stone.

But; *'the stone had gone, so had the one*
She came lookin' for
She runs to Simon Peter
'They've taken away the Lord'
Peter and John set off at a run

To where the body had lain
An empty grave, a hollow cave
And hope is born again'

The tomb was open and empty. Had Jesus been taken away? Or had he come back to life as he told them he would in words that sounded so strange at the time they didn't understand what he meant. In the story it seems that Peter and John had gone off to tell the other disciples. Mary was alone and overcome with bitter grief. She didn't know what was going on. She was out of her depth, out of resources. Exhausted by the events of previous days, emotionally and mentally overwhelmed, she did what any human being would do. She wept.

As she wept, she heard a voice she didn't recognize.

'Tell me lady, why do you weep
And who are you lookin' for'?

She thought it was the gardener, so

She turns towards the gardener
'I'm lookin' for the Lord'

And then the miracle; the word that instantly ended her pain and confusion and caused life and joy to rush back into her in a way she never imagined possible.

Just one word, she'd never heard
A melody so sweet
'Mary' was all he had to call
And she's kneelin' at his feet

Her Lord and friend, her Jesus, was alive, here with her at this very moment and speaking her own name. "Mary". All was well. Unbelievable, but very well! In this same encounter, an angel said to her *"why do you look for the living in the place of the dead.? Don't be alarmed. He is not here. He is risen. Go and tell the disciples and Peter. He is going ahead of you into Galilee. There you will see him, just as he told you' (Mark 16:6 NIV)*

Don't look for the living in the place of the dead
And don't let your sorrow erase what he said
And don't be discouraged, now the darkness had fled
Don't look for the living in the place of the dead'

Mary's sorrow melted, replaced by joy. Of course, news of this amazing kind spreads quickly. The next part of this incredible story is about to happen.

The news has spread "he's back from the dead'
But some say it can't be true
Disciples in confusion
They wait in an upper room
A voice says 'peace'; discussions cease
Every face turns white.
He said "do not fear, cause I'm really here
And everythin's alright!"

Now his followers were renewed in the passion and courage to continue to follow this new 'way' taught and demonstrated by this Jesus who arrived miraculously, lived astoundingly, died dramatically, came back to life mysteriously, appeared to hundreds, ate and drank with some of them, and said *'follow me'; do as I do; live as I live. And if you do, and believe in the way I am—believe in the True Life that is in me—you'll do even greater things than I do'*. That's another incredible statement.

In the Christian Scriptures, Jesus turned water into wine, walked on the lake, calmed a storm, fed 5000 by multiplying a few small loaves of bread and a few small fish, healed the sick and crippled, gave back sight to the blind, raised the dead to life, came back to life after being dead and buried for two days—and we'll do greater things! How do you get your head around that? And none of us can really know what he meant by that.

But what we can know by what Jesus said and did, is the kind of life to live and the way to live it. This is where we talk about the second aspect of not *'looking for the living in the place of the dead'*. And that is to separate our thinking about life from the physical-only component. Although we have physical requirements in order to continue living, these considerations are only part of our nature as human beings. Scriptures of every religion speak in similar terms. The Christian scriptures say it this way: *'God is Spirit and those who would worship must worship him in spirit and truth' (Bible: John 4:24)*. And *'man is made in the image of God, after his likeness' (Genesis 1:26.)* These statements, together with the lived experience of wisdom seekers throughout history, seem to be saying that we are spirit; that is our true nature. And, if we are spirit, then merely physical things cannot nourish and sustain us adequately.

So, to look only at the physical realm for understanding, guidance, meaning and purpose for our lives, is to *'look for the living in the place of the dead'*. What the wise of the ages are saying is that, like Jesus when he had risen from the dead, 'we are not there'. The true you and me are not to be found only in the physical places of this existence on earth. We are also beyond the physical; we are spirit. And, as we accept that reality, like Jesus we can rise to life in all its fullness; eternal life; breath by breath life in non-attachment to the constraints of time and space. Although that is not by any means my constant experience, I get sufficient glimpses of it to know it is true and to be encouraged onward.

This is the freedom, the salvation, Jesus says is available to all who seek it. Our greatest obstacle to experiencing this True Life, is our own egos. Big, tough, hard men and women in the jails of the world (and in prisons of various other kinds too) are saying, "I don't believe in God and religion; it's a crock of shit; just a crutch for people who are weak', etc. But the tragedy is that the ego is so inflated, it can't see. It's like a fat man who can't see over his belly to tie his shoes. The shoes are there. He just can't see them. The other side of the equation—and the razor wire, lights, dogs, bars, guards with guns—is the person living simply with spouse, children, family and community members, aware of his/her ordinariness and total reliance on the God who provides all that is. This person is humble and thankful for everything that comes to them in life. And they live in peace and joy knowing and accepting that every breath is a beautiful gift. They accept there is far greater wisdom than theirs, and humbly seek it day after day. And they learn and grow wise and good, kind and generous, loving and life-giving to all around them. They are in tune with creation. They know they are an ordinary part of the whole and, as they care for each tiny part of it, they care for themselves, every other person and all creatures. They enjoy everything that comes, changing what they can and accepting what they can't. And they're alive and a blessing to everyone around them. They don't need muscles or guns, because they fear nothing and want to destroy nothing. And they fear nothing because they experience themselves as one with all things; of the same elements and of the same Spirit. They simply 'are'.

When you compare the tough men and women in prisons of one kind or another who say ' God and religion is a lot of crap' with this person on the outside who we've just met, which of the two has a life that is working, is enjoyable and gives life to others? There's no comparison. And when Jesus said 'follow me', he didn't mean follow him to an organization characterised by religious jargon or mere mental assent to rules and regulations (although Jesus, himself, attended synagogues and religious festivals). He meant be like him—simple, focussed on Spirit, loving, giving, timeless, minimally using the physical things of the world, interdependent with everyone and everything, controlling noone and nothing, and moment by moment, breath by breath totally surrendered to God. He was pure being; fully human and fully divine. And, because he was pure being and beyond time and space, he remains pure being. He said we can be too. But we have to turn around 180 degrees. The way we are going, being, living, is leading only to death. In fact, as has been arged, we are already dead being primarily focussed only on that which is unable to give life. This focus underlies what, in Christian thinking, is called 'sin'. Rather than attempting a precise definition of sin, it is sufficient, for the purposes of this discussion, to suggest a couple of ideas we may consider further.

The word 'sin' in Spanish, means 'without'. I enjoy thinking about this fact because sin, as talked about in religious circles, tends to mean 'wrongdoing'. And doing is to do with physical. I think Jesus meant something far deeper than this. I think he was talking about 'wrong-being' that results from wrong thinking or wrong focus. Being who we truly are cannot be achieved without our conscious intent to experience ourselves as contained within the Spirit of God. To be 'without', ie, outside this Spirit reality, is not to be truly being. To be, is to be in Spirit. All of the self. The physical, emotional, psychological, spiritual being one with the great One behind and in and through every particle of the universe.

How can we know if what I've been saying here is valid? One way might be to look at the way political leaders and corporate bosses run things and consider the impact on the world: wars, destruction, oppression, borders, fear, self-aggrandisement, excesses for the diminishing few at the expense of the increasing many. Could we call this way death? Then we might look at the way of being behind every humanitarian agency throughout history: no borders, acceptance of all as brothers and sisters of equal worth, humility, generosity, surrender to a greater power, joy, peace, love. To be aware of the latter and yet somehow choose the former is perhaps the greatest human tragedy. How can this choice be explained? How is it that so many choose the former, and, tragically, by their choice make life difficult for themselves and others? We cannot not choose. We either choose death or we choose life.

Scripture says, *'choose this day whom you will serve'* (*Bible: Joshua 24:15*) Bob Dylan sang *"it may be the devil or it may be the Lord, but you're gonna have to serve somebody'.* The point is, service of good or evil, life or death, will happen whether we believe it or not. It's like gravity: it's just there. Not believing in it doesn't change its effect. It's essential for us to know that a choice will be made either deliberately or by default, and there will be consequences of both choice and non-choice. As intelligent beings, it makes sense to be as aware of our choices as possible. So, why is it that so many continue to look for life where it can't be found? Earlier we've talked about the ego and the True Self, and about allowing ourselves, either by ignorance or foolish rebellion, to remain ego-centred or to wake up and be transformed into our True Self. It may be that this is not news for you. I hope that is the case. But, if it isn't, and you're interested in moving from the constraints of the ego to the release of the True Self, there are many resources in wisdom literature and in the experience of the wise women and men through history that are available to us. At the end of this book I list some that I have found beneficial. They all start with finding ways to challenge and change our faulty thinking, and then move beyond the limits of the mind to become aware of our total being.

One small exercise you may like to try is this one from a Vietnamese monk, Thich Nhat Hanh. It is a two-breath meditation. As you draw breath in, think *'breathing in I calm my body'*. As you exhale that breath, think *'breathing out I smile'*. Drawing in the second breath, think *'Dwelling in the present moment'* and exhaling, think *'I know this is a wonderful moment'*.

Breathing in I calm my body
Breathing out I smile
Dwelling in the present moment
I know this is a wonderful moment.

(from Miracle of Mindfulness)

Chapter Four

Spirit and Fire

A voice shouting in the desert,
John was preparing a path for the Lord

He said I baptise you with water
To show you've repented, to show you've repented

He said one comes later, one far greater,
Even his sandals I'm unworthy to tie
One comes later, one far greater,
He will baptise you with spirit and fire,
Spirit and fire, spirit and fire.

He came to John in the Jordan,
So it would be as it was written

Jesus came up from the water,
The heavens were opened, the heavens were opened

The spirit came down like a dove
Alighted upon him, alighted upon him

A voice came loud from the heavens,
This is my son, he's my beloved

History isn't a good place to live. But it's a great place to visit. In the people and events of times past we can learn much of what we need to make our lives effective today. Although much in our world has changed with time, the essentials of our human condition—our striving, longing, hopes, fears, triumphs and joys—are probably not very different to those of many of our ancestors.

One of the most serious changes that seemed to be evident in our recent world was that everything had become profane. Somehow we allowed secular considerations of life to gain ascendancy over the wisdom and mystery undergirding all of creation. Our wonderful gifts of intellect, creativity and physical capability had ceased to refer to the reality of Spirit. In this movement away from what we may call Spirit of God, we lost the only point of reference that is able to make these abilities sacred and able to be used for good.

At this time in the history of planet earth, it could be argued that we need a reminder of who we are, where we came from, and what we're about as humans.

A story from about two thousand years ago might help.

The dad's name was Zechariah, and his wife's name was Elizabeth. They were good, upright folk who lived well. They were also quite old and didn't have any children. This was a matter of great sadness to them. Zechariah was a member of a group of priests who took turns to serve in the temple of the time. The customary way they got selected for temple duty was to draw straws. This particular day the lot fell to Zechariah. One of his duties was to burn incense. When it came time for this, and the assembled worshipers were praying outside, an angel appeared to Zechariah. Now, maybe you've been fortunate enough to have seen an angel. If you have, you will know how you felt. For the rest of us, we can only imagine. But it is reasonable to suggest that it would be a startling, unsettling event. This was the case with Zechariah. We are told he was *'startled and gripped with fear'*. You can read the whole story in the Gospel of Luke, chapter 1. You'll probably see something of yourself in this story.

'Don't be afraid' are words spoken hundreds of times in Scripture. The angel spoke them to Zechariah. And then the angel said, *'your prayer has been heard. Your wife, Elizabeth, will bear you a son, and you are to give him the name 'John'. He will be a joy and delight to you and many will rejoice because of his birth, for he will be great in the sight of the Lord. He is never to take wine or other fermented drink, and he will be filled with the Holy Spirit from birth. Many of the people of Israel will he bring back to the Lord their God. And he will go on before the Lord, in the spirit and power of Elijah, to turn the hearts of the fathers to their children, and the disobedient to the wisdom of the righteous—to make ready a people prepared for the Lord.*

Zechariah was a normal human being and said "*How can I be sure of this. I am and old man and my wife is well along in years.* The angel answered, *'I am Gabriel and stand in the presence of God, and I have been sent to speak to you and tell you of this good news. And now you will be silent and not able to speak until the day this happens because you did not believe my words, which will come true at their proper time'.*

So, the people were waiting outside for Zechariah and wondering why he stayed so long in the temple. And when he comes out he can't talk but makes signs to them and obviously looks like he's seen a vision. And when his time of duty was finished, he went home to Elizabeth. The story matter-of-factly says *'after this Elizabeth became pregnant and for five months stayed in seclusion. 'The Lord has done this for me'* she said. *'In these days he has shown his favour and taken away my disgrace among the people'.* The people in those days were just the same as we are—judgemental, critical, gossiping, harsh. A woman who couldn't bear children was treated as a second class citizen if that. As if the people who can produce children have anything to do with their own fertility! Some things don't change.

Then the story gets more interesting.

'In the sixth month, God sent the angel Gabriel to Nazareth, a town in Galilee, to a virgin pledged to be married to a man named Joseph, a descendent of David. The virgin's name was Mary. The angel went to her and said, 'greetings you who are highly favoured! The Lord is with you.' As you would imagine, *'Mary was greatly troubled at these words and wondered what kind of greeting this might be. And the angel said to her 'Don't be afraid, Mary, you have found favour with God. You will be with child and will give birth to a son, and you are to give him the name Jesus. He will be great and will be called the Son of the Most High . . . and his kingdom will never end'. Mary said, 'How will this be, since I am a virgin'? The angel answered, 'The Holy Spirit will come upon you and the power of God will overshadow you so the holy one to be born will be called the Son of God'.*

The angel went on to say that Mary's cousin, Elizabeth, who was barren, is going to have a child in her old age, that she's already in her sixth month, and that for God nothing is impossible. *"I am the Lord's servant' Mary said. "May it be to me as you have said'.*

The story of this connected family gets more amazing. Mary gets ready and hurries off to the hill country in Judea to visit her cousin, Elizabeth. When Mary enters Zechariah's house and Elizabeth hears her greeting, the baby *'leaps in her womb and Elizabeth is filled with the Holy Spirit'.*(Luke chapter 1 . . . read it all!)

When the baby was born and the people expected him to be named Zechariah after his father, Elizabeth spoke up and said, *"No; his name is John'.* As if the woman wasn't to be taken seriously, they asked Zechariah. *He called for a writing tablet and wrote 'his name is John'. At that moment, his tongue was loosed and could speak again!* This is no ordinary event. God is here in power. And when God says something, it seems like it's a good idea to take notice!

Thirty years later this 'miracle' baby, John, born to an old and barren woman, becomes John the Baptist. It seems this prophet was born for the primary purpose of announcing the arrival of Jesus Christ in a way that would not go unnoticed. More about that soon. Although his second cousin by blood, John willingly served Jesus as his Lord, and passionately asserted that Jesus was the revealed Lord of all. This Jesus, John said, *is 'the one who comes later, one who is greater than me; even his sandals I'm unworthy to tie'.* The song *Spirit and Fire* is about this powerful event in history that affects all humanity before and since and for all time to come. It unfolded something like this.

John had always been a man of the Spirit. He didn't walk to society's tune; he followed the inner voice of God that had been with him from before birth. Being unlike much of the world, he chose to live simply and ascetically out in the desert. He wasn't into mortgages and white goods (or the equivalent of the day); his only desire was to obey the voice of God that spoke within him. John's coming onto the world stage was anticipated by another prophet, Isaiah, about 700 years earlier. *'A voice of one calling in the wilderness: Prepare the way for the Lord; make straight paths for him. Every valley shall be filled in, every mountain and hill made low. The crooked roads shall become straight, the rough ways smooth. And all mankind will see God's salvation' (Bible: Isaiah 40: 3-5)*

When a king was making a journey in his own country or to another country, the roads he would travel were worked on to make them smoother and more appropriate for him. In this case of John preparing a path for the Lord—for his King—his preparation was of a moral and spiritual nature. He focussed on the need for people to recognize and turn away from wrong behaviour, and towards a 'right' state of being—a state which acknowledged both the need for transformation, and for a saviour who could provide that.

But back to John. These days we'd call him eccentric or crazy, and either have nothing to do with him, or lock him up in a psych ward. But in truth, the people to whom John was preaching were the true eccentrics; they had moved away from their centre—their God-Spirit nature. Paradoxically, John was one of the few who were 'concentric', that is, he was perfectly in tune and in balance with his centre which is the image of God within him. That is the Centre to which he said we must return.

Here was this hairy, bearded, wild-looking man wearing nothing but animal skins and rough, handmade sandals, and living in the desert on honey and possibly carob seeds. John was fiercely committed to telling it how it was revealed to him by the Spirit of God. He wasn't concerned about what people thought of him; their opinions were irrelevant. Many were going the wrong way, their way led to death and destruction, and the only way to live was to turn around and go the other way—the way of righteousness; the way of God.

That was around A.D. thirty. To look around us at the state of the world today, one would have to conclude that our need for a major turn around is no less now than it was then. In fact, it's likely that the need is even greater today. The expansion of our knowledge and ability to manipulate the natural world has seduced us into a very dangerous position of thinking we can do this very well on our own; we have become more arrogant and proud than ever. When the correction comes to us—as corrections always do—our distress will be correspondingly dramatic.

So who are the '*voices shouting in the desert*' today? Who are the voices of wisdom; the voices of caution and guidance? They are few but they are here. They are those who dare to continue to speak the ancient truths of Scripture and other wisdom literature and tradition. They are heard in many religious, non-government and academic circles. They are sacrificially loving all who have no-one to love them. They are the ones giving and serving and caring in a world that has forgotten the value of these qualities or, at least, dismissed these as of less value than science, technology, and the market economy.

Growth and development have become almost exclusively external to the human person. They are to do with producing, consuming, gaining and using information and skills and modifying environments. They are to do with creating artificial ones in their places, and producing wastes of all kinds—some nuclear waste with half-lives of hundreds of thousands of years that no-one really knows what to do with. Nor do we know the eventual effects on the planet.

Much of what we promote as success is failure. Much of what we are proudest about is obscene and shameful. In these days we are taking food grains from those who have very little else, and using it to fuel industry, and to provide luxuries for a diminishing number of citizens in so-called 'first-world' nations. Still more obscene are those involved in the process of patenting food grains rendering the staples of life available only to those who can pay.

But how has this grotesque distortion of humankind been accomplished; how has it been allowed to occur and spread like a cancer? There is no short answer to this sad illusion of success into which we have fallen. But there are some clues that we could consider if we are interested in committing ourselves to becoming life-givers to the world.

What are these clues? There are two I'd like to mention that are to do with the staples of physical life: bread and water. And not just bread and water as commonly understood, but another kind of bread and another kind of water.

In our world there is reality we can see and there is reality we can't see. We can see trees and other green plants, but we can't see the oxygen they produce which we know to be real because it keeps us alive. In chapter 6 of John's Gospel, there's a story about these two kinds of bread that we need to read and understand. You may remember the Jewish Exodus story of about 1250 BC. What kept them alive was 'manna'—a kind of bread that came down from 'heaven' each day, was found on the ground, and was picked up and eaten by these travellers in the wilderness. The bread couldn't be kept or it would go rotten. They had to trust God to provide it each day, and God did just that.

In the story in John's Gospel, people were following Jesus around because he had just fed five thousand with five small barley loaves and two small fishes that a boy happened to have. People were more interested in a free lunch than anything else, and Jesus knew this full well. So he said to them, *I tell you the truth; you are looking for me because saw miraculous signs and because you ate the loaves and had your fill. Do not work for food that spoils but for food that endures to eternal life, which the Son of Man will give you.* So the people asked him *What miraculous sign will you give that we may see it and believe you?* (Remember he's just fed five thousand of them) *What will you do? Our forefathers ate manna in the desert; as it is written: he gave them bread from heaven to eat'.* Jesus said to them, *I tell you the truth, it is not Moses who has given you bread from heaven, but it is my father who gives the true bread from heaven. For the bread of God is he who comes down from heaven and gives life to the world.*

Digest this for a bit: there is manna bread—physical stuff that they ate and it kept their bodies alive; and there is 'true bread'. Jesus went on to say *'I am the bread of life; he who comes to me will never be hungry and he who believes in me will never be thirsty' (John 6:35)*. Somehow, mysteriously, Jesus was offering a different kind of life that relied not on physical bread and water but on the 'unseen' mystery that is the power of Life in him that, with our willingness, could become the power of Life in us too. The bread we see gives life to the bodies we see; the Bread we don't see gives Life to our deep, inner True Selves we don't see.

The second clue I'd like to explore occurred in history before the first. Though the two belong together because they are part of the same 'life-giving system' taught and demonstrated by the historical Jesus.

A line from this song, *'Spirit and Fire'*, gives a clue to how we may continue developing our awareness of the two ways we can be and go. John the Baptist says it: *'I baptise you with water (external, physical, material) . . . but one comes later . . . he will baptise you with Spirit and fire' (internal, spiritual, non-material) (Mark 1:3)*.

In the modern world, we have been seduced into believing that the external, physical, material world in and of itself is reality. Yet it is a part of reality only insofar as it is considered in reference to it's origins in God. To the extent that the physical world is considered without such reference to God, it is illusion and not real at all. This can be difficult for us to grasp. There is more to Reality than we will see in this life. Scripture says *'we see now as in a glass darkly; then we will see face to face' (1 Corinthians 13:12)*. Our selling out—inadvertent or wilful—to this illusion, prevents us from experiencing the fullness of life that God has for us in the Spirit. Without deferring to God we have no real life.

So, there's baptism with the ordinary wet stuff for the physical life and as a sign of the Spiritual, and there's baptism with different stuff; spirit and fire, for the interior life that is ever present, beyond space and time, and formless.

There are many references to the 'living water'—the 'spirit and fire' referred to in this John the Baptist story. Once Jesus asked a Samaritan woman drawing water from a well if she would give him a drink. They had a bit of dialogue about him being a Jew and asking her, a Samaritan (the two groups didn't associate culturally), for a drink. In this conversation Jesus said to her, '*If you knew the gift of God and who it is who asks you for a drink, you would have asked him and he would have given you living water*'). Jesus is talking about spiritual reality. The woman's response indicates she's stuck in physical unreality. In her mind water is wet stuff, it's down the well, and you need a bucket and rope with which to get it to the surface. Jesus pushes the point a bit further when he says '*Everyone who drinks (well) water will be thirsty again, but whoever drinks the water I give will never thirst. Indeed, the water I give him (her) will become in him (her) a spring of water welling up to eternal life*'

The conversation went on a bit and the woman asked Jesus for this 'living water' so she didn't have to keep coming to the well every day. She hadn't got the point yet but, like most of us, wanted the easy way out of the daily struggle. She mentioned that the Samaritans worshiped God on this mountain but the Jews worship God in Jerusalem. Jesus went on; he wanted her to understand the difference between the Spirit reality and the physical reality. '*Believe me woman, the time is coming when you will worship the father neither on this mountain nor in Jerusalem . . . a time is coming and has now come* (with his arrival) *when the true worshipers will worship the father in spirit and truth, for they are the kind of worshipers the father seeks. God is spirit and his worshipers must worship him in spirit and in truth'*. The woman knew that *'the Messiah, called Christ, is coming, and he will explain everything to us'*. Jesus said *I who speak to you am he'*. You can read the whole story in John's Gospel, chapter 4.

Here is an example of the call to us all to choose where we stand on the life-death continuum. Are we stuck like the woman in a mindset that conceives only of physical, material life? Or are we prepared, with some encouragement from Wisdom lived and expounded by Jesus and others, to open ourselves to the possibility of there being another way to be. The world is dying because it has, in large part, refused to consider any other way than that of material being. Many have been baptised with water, including the so-called Christian peoples of the world who constantly wage war on their brothers and sisters. Jesus said *'love your enemies and pray for those who persecute you'(Bible: Matthew 5:44)'*. How can we claim to be his followers while we fear and hate and kill our enemies, most of whom are defenceless women and children? Could it be that we in these probably well-meaning but deluded societies need the baptism to which John referred; the one of 'spirit and fire'? Judging by Jesus' requirement to love God and ones neighbor as oneself, it would seem so.

In hanging onto the only life we know, we deny ourselves access to the rest of Reality. If we settle for the common well-water of this time-limited physical-only life, we deny ourselves the exhilarating rush of constantly refreshing, living water of time-unlimited spirit life; eternal life—life unconstrained by the limits of time and space. Why any of us would knowingly settle for distress when we could have bliss is beyond me. But I do and we do.

The words of this little song, *'Spirit and Fire'*, lifted fairly much straight from Scripture, are one expression of the answer to many of the ills of this world and our lives in it. There was a voice of wisdom and life speaking in the desert of deception and death. In the case of John, he was on a mission. He'd been sent ahead of Jesus to wake up and open up hearts and minds that had been closed and hardened by the concerns of the common life. Today there seem to be too few preparing the way. Where there are no sign-posts we get easily lost—either in the external desert of distractions, or the interior desert of fantasy.

I recently experienced first hand the value of sign-posts in the literal desert of Western Australia. My friend, Howard, and I—and his friend, Ade—travelled the 1900 kilometre Canning Stock Route (CSR) starting at Wiluna north of the Wheatbelt, and ending at Hall's Creek in the Kimberley. The entire journey is on natural formation dirt. For the most part, there is no road. The route crosses about one thousand sand dunes varying from 8 to 15 metres in height, and with distances between them varying from a few hundred metres to a couple of kilometres. It traverses both the Little Sandy Desert and the Great Sandy Desert. This route varies from 2 wheel ruts to a several-vehicle-wide scar, to vast salt pans where you can make your own track. Most of it is heavily corrugated sand or gravel, gibbers (a litter of small, sharp rocks as far as the eye can see), stoney creek beds, or clay.

Talk about the need for sign-posts. In 1900 kilometres there is one community where you can purchase fuel, have a shower or toilet and make a phone call. There aren't many sign-posts because there's nothing much to point to. But the sign posts that are there—mostly rusty pieces of flattened, once-corrugated iron or weather-faded scraps of wood on which is roughly hand painted 'CSR'—are invaluable. Without these you could take a side—track, get lost and die of thirst before you were found.

The inner desert of the human soul is similar to the Canning Stock Route, and similarly in need of signs to keep us on the track. And today, as much as any time in history, we need signs—people who have travelled the road and know enough of it to help direct us safely. John the Baptist was one such sign.

John was preaching repentance—that churchy word for 'doing a u-ey' or a '180'; turning around and going the opposite way to the way you've been going. He talked about 'sin'—an unpopular word today meaning being out of step with God/Love. And he talked about the fact that we need to acknowledge that we've been out of step, we need to feel lousy about that, and we need to know that we need forgiveness for our wrong living so we can go on in new life unhindered and totally free, no matter what our circumstances are.

So the baptism with water was an outward sign that we had turned around. It was an outward sign of the reality that we had also been forgiven and were free. The *One who comes later,* Jesus himself, was going to baptise us—immerse, soak, and fill us—in his transcendent, Spirit Reality within and beyond the bounds of physical material, time and space. Unless we comprehend the need and enter into this Great Spirit Reality, the ills of the world will not change one iota.

We see the story of Jesus coming to the Jordan to be baptised by John as foreshadowed by the prophet, Isaiah, 700 years earlier, and even earlier in Psalm 2. This wasn't just an unusual Sunday afternoon down by the river. This was a momentous, life-altering action of the One True God of the universe. '*He came to John in the Jordan, so it would be as it was written* all those hundreds of years earlier. *The Spirit came down like a dove and alighted upon him. A voice came from heaven saying, 'this is my son, my beloved, in whom I delight. I will put my spirit on him and he will bring justice to the nations* (Isaiah 42).

These are great words of life changing and life giving. Not to engage with this action of God which took place and has implications for us personally, is to remain separated from Truth; separated from our True Selves, from each other, from the natural world and from God. This is serious separation! This is the separation we are experiencing and hearing about in much of the trouble in our world. Behind every suffering, every piece of damage, every abuse, every violation, is the reality of this separation.

There is no other way to live well than to become immersed in—become one with—this great power of love and life and *Spirit and fire*. Our cleverness won't do it. Our physical strength won't do it. Our human ego won't do it. Only our centre—our heart and soul—united in the great Centre of All is able to set right what is wrong and return us to life where there is now death. United in this Oneness, we can experience freedom even whilst imprisoned in any of the prisons we manufacture for ourselves, or which are manufactured for us by a society that has lost its way.

. . . .

Chapter Five

As A Doe

As a doe longs for running streams,
So longs my soul for you my God

My soul is thirsting for the God of Life,
When shall I see him face to face
I have no food but tears day and night,
And men say 'where is your God'

I remember and my soul melts within,
I'm on my way to the house of God
Among cries of joy and praise,
Place your trust in God

Why so downcast, oh my soul,
Why do you sigh so deep within
Place your hope in the God of life,
I shall praise him again

When I find my soul downcast within,
I think of you, oh Mt Zion

Deep calls to deep as your waters roar,
Over me all your waves pour

Copyright: Mike Fitzgerald GIA.Pub. 1973

I n the introduction you read this:
'For, though God be everywhere present, yet he is only present to thee in the deepest and most central part of thy soul . . . etc. And also:

Man has no rest until he finds his rest in God' (St Augustine)

These short statements hold the key to fullness of life—to true freedom, to peace, to joy. In these statements lived, there is release from effects of everything life can bring to us. St Paul alluded to this when he said *'I have learned to be satisfied in all circumstances; whether I am hungry or well fed, it is all the same to me' (Bible: Philippians 4:12)*

He had learned the secret of life—to find his rest in the life-giving mystery that is God in the ever—present moment.

Isn't it true that you have a longing inside you for something more; for release from suffering, loneliness, fear; for an experience of peace and quiet joy? Isn't that true for you? It is for me and every other human being I have met and with whom I have discussed the important things of this mysterious experience called life.

As I mentioned in another place, my own soul-longing began when I was quite young. I don't have any neat theological ideas about how (or if) God 'calls' or 'chooses'. I just know from my own experience that it seems God does! Whether we are chosen from the womb or not, I don't know. It seems unfair for one to be chosen and another not. I am confident that the God of Love in whom I believe is not capricious. As Scripture requires us not to be partial, it's a given that God is not

partial either. '*the wisdom that comes from heaven is first of all pure;
then peace-loving, considerate, submissive, full of mercy and good fruit,
impartial and sincere.(Bible: James:3.17)*

In John's Gospel, Jesus says *"you did not choose me, but I have
chosen you and appointed you to go and bear fruit—fruit that will last'
(Bible: John 15:16)* Here he was talking to the disciples. Clearly he *chose*
them from the countryside for the beginning of his world-transforming
mission. Later, St Peter talks about all who believe as '*a chosen people,
a royal priesthood, a holy nation, a people belonging to God that you
may declare the praises of him who called you out of darkness into his
wonderful light' (Bible: 1Peter 2:9)*

So, if God is impartial, and those who hear and believe are 'chosen',
then all who hear are chosen, but some refuse the offer. Of course there
are many who haven't had the opportunity to hear. That's another matter
and not for discussion here.

I was reluctant and accepted the offer at first for all the wrong
reasons. For a good while I was scared of 'burning in hell', whatever
that may mean. So I was 'good' because I was afraid. We are supposed
to be good because we are 'in-love', ie, connected to God. For me that
came a lot later. Over a couple of decades my connection with God
moved slowly from my head to include my heart. I knew from things
my mind had heard and taken on. Now I know from an inner knowledge
that has accumulated and deepened over time. Yet for all those years
there has been the struggle. It hasn't been a dream run by any measure.
I have doubted, railed, submitted, sorrowed, been highly anxious,
deeply depressed (and medicated) and I've experienced being on the
mountain-top on occasions too. The tension is still here, although these
days I am far more relaxed about 'what is'; even though I seem to be
really 'slow', I have begun to learn that God is in all things and all
things are, somehow, OK; all is always well. I am learning to be aware

and present to this moment. This is where God meets me; not yesterday or tomorrow or when I'm 'holy' or whatever, but here and now and it is good. It is all good.

I'm glad God bothered me enough for me to hear the call and respond. What I find sad, is so many have heard and turned away, or heard incorrectly, or haven't heard the truth at all. Perhaps those with the message have failed to get it out in a way that is receivable. I feel the pain of my brothers and sisters whose lives demonstrate that they haven't been able, for whatever reason, to respond and live. I don't know how anyone struggling can go on facing life day after day with nothing deeper than themselves or their daily horoscope for guidance and nourishment.

The deep longing in me continues long after knowing that its satisfaction has begun and will only be complete when I am completely one with God. That's the great mystery. It is almost certain that will not happen in my lifetime on earth. And that's OK too.

This beautiful song taken from Psalm 42 that begins (paraphrased),

As a doe longs for running streams, so longs my soul for you my God.
My soul is thirsting for the God of life

This inner hunger and thirst—this longing—is at the centre of every human being's experience of life—whether acknowledged or not. If it's true that we are made in the image of God and after God's likeness—and many religious traditions, much wisdom literature dealing with humankind, accepts something like this transcendent mystery at the centre of reality—then we are hard-wired for engagement with this mystery that we call God. We cannot *not* seek engagement with God and be fully alive. We can kid ourselves that we are OK without 'that religious stuff' and, in doing so, inadvertently deny ourselves access to the very life we think we already have; the 'I'm OK' idea put about by popular psychology. And, in a way, this idea is true; we are OK. As we are, we are gloriously made, and possess all we need to live fully and well.

The way in which this idea is 'not ok' (and, therefore, we are not ok), is in the delusion that my thinking, reasoning mind, my physical body, and my emotions are who I am, and that I am the master of my own destiny. Here is the problem that is being played out on the world stage by the majority of sports, film, recording and media stars, entrepreneurs, fashion leaders, political leaders and, sadly, many leaders of the popular, rapidly growing churches that promote the gospel of 'prosperity' in material terms. The power behind all of this is the immature, human ego; the little 'me' part of us. When we become truly 'OK', is when we wake up and see that this ego is the lesser part of the self, and that there is a greater part; a truer part; a part that is capable of attaining insight, wisdom, authentic humanity. This has been called by many the 'True Self'. Thomas Aquinas called it the 'Universal Reason—the Law of the Universe'. Others call it the Spirit Reality at the centre of our being that is beyond feeling, beyond thinking and beyond reasoning. Although these abilities are wonderful and make up rich aspects of the total human being, they are not the whole truth about us. Truth (God) can only be found beyond them; past them; deeper than them. One wisdom tradition says *'beyond the senses is the mind, beyond the mind is reason, and beyond reason is Truth'*

Another puts it this way: *'Science is the lowest form of human knowledge—the knowledge of the material world through discursive reason. Philosophy is above science, because it goes beyond the material world and explores the world of thought, but it is still confined to discursive reason. Theology is above philosophy, because it is open*

to the world of transcendent reality, but its methods are still those of science and philosophy. It is only wisdom that can transcend reason and know the Truth, not discursively but intuitively, not by its reflection in the world of the senses but in its Ground, where knowing is also being.'
(Bede Griffiths: Return to the Centre)

It seems really difficult for us to abandon our firmly held beliefs gained from lifetimes of conditioning. Through history we have experienced the battle between these opposing inner forces of ego self and True Self; between senses, mind, reason, and God. Our True Self longs for union with God. And we cannot be satisfied with anything less. We distract ourselves with all sorts of noise, activity and achievement. We esteem wealth, beauty, power, and intellect because they seem to our egos to be the projection of who humans can be. We make heroes of those who excel in these areas of human ability, and deify them because it's the only kind of glory many are able to see in this world. Acting this way is at least a suggestion of what we intuitively know is available to us. But we either don't believe it possible for us, personally or, at least, we haven't experienced it yet. And the degree of deity ascribed to the various 'heroes' is indicated by the millions of dollars their skill attracts; the players of football, baseball, tennis, formula one racing car drivers, moto GP riders, etc. And the true heroes—those who give, serve, guide, protect, honour—are neither recognized nor remunerated for their humanity of excellence. We have removed ourselves far from our True Selves.

But it is this true part that is hungry and thirsty and continues to long for satisfaction.

As a doe longs for running streams
So longs my soul for you my God
My soul is thirsting for the God of life

When will I see him face to face
I have no food but tears day and night
And men say where is your God

The human soul is thirsting for the inexpressible mystery of God. We are not talking about some religious institution developed over centuries my men and women—sadly, mostly men and, therein, lies much of the problem. The creative, intuitive, feminine, nurturing aspects of humanity have been denied because males have taken charge and dismissed those life-giving human qualities as irrelevant or, certainly, inferior to the intellectual and physical abilities. Much of such institutional tradition bears little resemblance to the life-giving mystery of that which we are here calling God. And yet, the religious organizations of the world have played, and continue to play, an essential role in presenting humankind with the reality of Spirit. Without the commitment of people of faith, the world would be a very much darker place than it is.

Those who are serious about their belief in the mystery of life understand the tormented experience of the writer of this psalm; *I have no food, but tears day and night, and men say 'where is your God'*. It is not possible to truly seek God in comfort. Anything easily won seems of little real value. It is only through suffering and desolation—which include our modern epidemic of distress, depression, despair—that endurance is produced and developed; it is only through endurance that character and profound human maturity is created. So, the experience of *'tears day and night'* is an essential, if unpleasant, section of the road to Life.

As a doe longs for running streams, so longs my soul for you my God.

I remember and my soul melts within, I'm on my way to the house of God
Among cries of joy and praise, place your trust in God

The writer remembers the road he's on and why. It is the only road worth travelling. All others are, literally, dead ends; all others lead to a shallow experience of life, nothing of value being achieved, a living destruction and death. Only the road to God offers life and peace, and joy with struggles that attend it as a matter of course.

Whether the '*house of God*' is a human-built place of worship or not, doesn't matter. The tiniest particle of matter in the universe is a house of God who is its life, its form, its purpose. As we realize this, *cries of joy and praise* spring unbidden from the deepest parts of our souls and bodies. To have this lived experience of God is bliss. This is what we are designed for. This is our natural state. This is the state from which we separated ourselves when we gained the 'knowledge' that we could be masters of our own destinies. And that is illusion. There are only two options: either we willingly surrender our freedom to God and, paradoxically, receive true freedom—Scripture says '*if you die you will live' (Bible: Matthew 16:25)*—or remain a slave to the unconscious forces within the self—the desire, fear, ego. We don't have the option of being masters of anything; either we are slaves to the ego and securely bound, or we are slaves to God and freed to fly unhindered.

Among cries of joy and praise
Place your trust in God

Trust is generally misunderstood. We talk about 'gaining a person's trust' or 'trusting a person'. The fact is no human being is wholly trustworthy. Sooner or later, everyone will let us down in some way. No matter how loving and faithful you believe you are, you are not perfect and, thus, not able to be perfectly trustworthy; you will let someone down at some time. Trust is not something to be put wholly in another person. There are two dangers with trying to put your complete trust in someone.

First, you could be putting responsibility for your wellbeing and security in the hands of another fallible human being (just like you) and failing to be responsible for yourself. Secondly, you could be placing an unreasonable expectation and burden on the other, possibly causing them to feel pressured, and likely causing you grief when they let you down.

Nowhere in wisdom literature does it say '*trust one another*'. It does say *love one another,* and love doesn't place burdens upon us; love frees us. So, what about trust? I believe that as we surrender to God who is Love, and learn to love, we become so secure within that way of being that we easily choose to *entrust* ourselves to one another. In doing so, we may be aware that we could be let down and hurt. But we can choose to accept that if it comes as a normal part of being in authentic relationship with others; always a risky business.

The only one wholly trustworthy is God

Why so downcast, oh my soul
Why do you sigh so deep within?

Then remembering . . .

Place your hope in the God of life
I will praise him again!

Life brings us a rich variety of emotional experiences. As long as we live, we are both ego-self and True-Self. Which of the two we choose to follow dictates the patterns and extent of what we experience. If we give free rein to the conscious and unconscious forces of the ego, we will likely experience being tossed this way and that with great frequency and magnitude; we will often be disturbed and tormented. For example, if you really want the day to be fine and it's raining, if you want someone to like you and they don't, if you hope for anything that you have no control over, you will be downcast. If something good happens, you're up; if something bad happens, you're down. What an insecure and ridiculous way to live your life. And yet, so many of us do and remain downcast, despairing, anxious.

Why so downcast, oh my soul
Why do you sigh so deep within?

It may be because of one of these negative outcomes that you set up for yourself by putting your hope in the wrong thing; in something of the physical world to satisfy your senses, mind or reason. Or you may be downcast because of your soul's deep longing for God that cannot be completely satisfied in this world. Either way, the reminder is to

Place your hope in the God of life
I will praise him again!

The refrain is the ever-present, inner hunger and thirst that we must practise allowing rather than avoiding by one distraction or another. It is not 'strong' to have and not acknowledge this need; it is in us all. We are all weak until it is satisfied, and nothing on earth can satisfy it. Everyone who is either unaware of this need or refuses to recognize and acknowledge its validity is in deep, personal trouble. When such people are in positions of political, religious, economic or other kind of power or influence, the personal trouble becomes communal and may become national and international trouble. We are experiencing that in our world today. Where there is wisdom, it is not being sought and followed; where there ought to be wisdom there is little.

There are too few people heeding the inner longing for God. As a result, they and all around them suffer an insatiable hunger and an unquenchable thirst. This soul-longing is not just an optional extra, or a 'crutch for weak people'; this is life or death for individuals, nations, species and the entire planet. This is normal. What is abnormal is to deny it, ridicule it, resist it, distract ourselves to quieten the inner promptings, believe we can do it on our own. Look around you. What do you see? Sustainable life, peace and harmony between people and nations, equity, simplicity, compassion, generosity? What do you see in yourself? Is everything OK? Or, perhaps, you see more confused struggle than you'd like.

As a doe longs for running streams, so longs my soul for you my God

Although this is the utterance of a man who has acknowledged and submitted his life to God, he has experienced both the joy and the suffering of this common life. Even those who have chosen to live their lives in accordance with the love revealed in Scripture are not exempt from all that life holds. They do, however, have a higher vantage point from which to see correctly and react differently from those without this view. When we intuitively discern the paradox of life—that less is more, that weak is strong, that loss is gain, that surrender is release—then we are enabled to embrace both the pleasant and the unpleasant with greater equanimity.

When I find my soul downcast within, I think of you, oh Mt Zion
Deep calls to deep as your waters roar, over me all your waves pour

In these final lines of the song to God, we hear the singer downcast yet thinking of the 'high places'—the dwelling place of God. There are many interpretations of *'deep calls to deep and your waters roar, over me all your waves pour'*. These include literal rain water torrents rushing down an actual mountain, torrents from the 'deep' above the earth from where all rain comes, ocean waves powerfully overwhelming all in their path. However, perhaps a more useful way to consider these lines is in light of the fact that the truth alluded to throughout God-inspired Scripture is more allegory, metaphor and myth than history; even in the historically accurate parts, there is layer upon layer of meaning for us to plumb with our souls and our minds.

I am here defining myth as 'something that never was but always is'. Another paradox perhaps? But I suggest there is far more benefit for us to focus on the 'always is' part.

Life is. God is. We can't define any of these in terms that are anywhere near adequate. This is the great value of considering these difficult realities as myth; we can't neatly find slots for them and file them away; we are left with the tension that requires our 'at-tension'. And as we attend, the obscuring cloud thins and allows us glimpses of the 'beyond' that nourish us and call us ever onward in our inner-longing to be and know and be known so we can rest.

In line with these suggestions, it is probably helpful for us to consider *'deep calls to deep'* as the deep, obscure and mysterious but real presence of God calling to that 'deep', God-part of me; my True-Self. This is the part of every human that needs to be allowed to expand and take gentle, powerful precedence over all else in us. Then, when *'over me all your waves pour'*, we are one with the waves and, although overwhelmed, are not destroyed; rather, we are melted in to the Great Water and are at home and at rest whilst in this life, and, eternally. We are called to *'set our minds on things that are above, not on earthly things. For we have died, and our lives are hidden with Christ in God' (Bible: Colossians 3:2-3)* This is not an encouragement to willingly end our own lives. Rather it is an encouragement to live with our priorities set correctly. In all Scriptures and wisdom literature, this is the centrepiece; release yourself from attachment to life as you know it in order to find life as it really is.

Chapter Six

Travel Far and Wide

Early morning light can be deceiving,
The rising sun reveals the risen one
Shadows on the lake their patterns weaving,
Standing by the shore God's only son

Every eye is staring at the shoreline,
The lord is here, the whisper goes around
They come ashore eat fish and bread together,
And Jesus says to Peter 'hear me now'.

Peter feed my sheep, Peter don't be weak,
Follow me wherever that road may lead
Peter do you love me, and nothing else above me,
If you do then feed my sheep

Time has come when Jesus must be leaving
He tells them of the holy one to come
A gift of love to all of his disciples,
To give them strength to do what must be done

Travel far and wide, tell them why I died,

And make disciples everywhere you go

Baptising everyone in the Father, Spirit, Son,

And I'll always be with you evermore

Copyright: Garth Hewitt

My wife, Jenny, and her mother, Lomonde, want to check something out at a small shopping centre in Woodlands-Wembley Downs—one of Perth's western-most suburbs on the beautiful West Australian coast.

The morning is sunny and warm, the breeze is almost non-existent. The shopping centre backs onto the Anglican church of St Paul, where my father and mother attended worship in their retirement years, and experienced what was, for them, a new kind of experience of God and of belonging in that little faith community. Here, my dear old mum—who had been very traditional in her faith and restrained in her ways for most of her life—was frequently heard to say 'praise the Lord'. It was wonderful that, towards the end of their lives, mum and dad experienced a freshness and new joy in their spirits. St Paul's is also the church where I last saw my mum and dad; both their funeral services were held here.

As I'm not particularly interested in shopping, I take the opportunity to revisit those final moments with mum and dad who crossed over from this life 23 and 15 years ago respectively.

I decide to go into this little church and just sit in the quietness of this holy space, muted sunlight streaming through three, floor to vaulted-ceiling narrow windows on the eastern wall, and brilliantly lighting the beautiful, circular, stained-glass window in the west end of the south wall behind the altar. Some folk are chattering happily in the hall behind me as they attend to the business of setting out and arranging a mass of donated domestic goods for a huge jumble sale.

Outside the wall of glass on the west side of the auditorium is a small, paved courtyard enclosed by a cream brick wall simply dressed in red bougainvillea and white climbing roses. Beyond the wall are peppermint trees, and acacias wearing golden blossom. As my eyes and mind travel further, I glimpse the shopping centre through the peppermint trees. Behind them are houses that give way to scrubby bush reserve, West Coast Highway and the great Indian Ocean.

Sitting here remembering mum and dad, and travelling in my heart and mind to a variety of places, it occurs to me that this place is called the Church of St Paul the Evangelist. It's also the final church of my mum and dad who started me on this quest by being on the same quest themselves. And I'm writing about the Garth Hewitt song, *'Travel Far and Wide (tell them why I died).'* I clearly know that I am in exactly the right place, and I feel excited beyond what is normal for me. There's something different and special about this moment. As I sit here and write, I'm not sure where I'm going with this piece, but I have a strong sense of aliveness in my soul that is taking me where I am meant to go.

My own desire has been, for as many years as I can remember, to travel towards the mystery of life that we call God; nothing unusual in that. I believe that every human being is imbued with this inner stamp of God and, as St Augustine and so many others have observed, *'we have no rest until we find our rest in God'.*

For the past thirty-five years I have been passionately and actively engaged in this quest to seek, to question, find and lose again and again, discuss, sing about, pray about and study this whole business of the spiritual path for me. It is the single most important endeavour of my life. Without this being right, nothing else can be right. It's like a young child learning the letters in order to make later sense of words.

'*Travel far and wide, tell them why I died*' is the requirement—the command—of God through the person of Jesus Christ to all who believe in the One True God and the Son whom God sent for our benefit. More on that soon. But, when we look at what's happening in the world today, it is pretty obvious that the way we're doing life is pretty much a failure. When Gandhi was asked '*what do you think of the civilization of America*'? he is reported to have said, '*I think it would be a very good idea*'. But I'm not singling out the U.S. for any special treatment in regard to being 'uncivil'; the U.S., together with every other developing, western style nation has both wonderful desirable qualities, as well as diabolical ones. And our bad habits of self-focus, rampant consumerism, etc, are no longer limited to the western nations. China, India and many other eastern and central cultures are, sadly, taking on the worst of the western habits. In addition to the natural environment, what is suffering in this shift in focus and motivation is the spiritual centre of the human being. Is humanity becoming more profane? Have we all but sold out to the lie of the 'free' markets and consumerism, and the trinkets of the physical world?

I deliberately use the word 'developing' for the U.S., Australia, the U.K., Western Europe and many other nations aspiring to the western way. By the standard of universal wisdom, these nations have barely begun developing in ways that truly matter to humankind. I refer here to the single way of being human that works; the way of Love. Many worthy volumes have been written on the subject of Love, and I neither intend to, nor am I capable of, writing such a volume. Instead I would like to offer a few signs of love that may help our consideration of its central place in life. Love prefers to give than to take. Love prefers simplicity to complexity. Love prefers gentleness over a show of strength. Love is involved with bringing life and light where there is death and darkness. Love prefers to create and sustain than to destroy and deplete. For more indications, you may like to read the passage known and treasured by many in St Paul's first letter to the early Christians in the city of Corinth. (see 1 Corinthians chapter 13)

My mum and dad—Carol and Lance—were good solid, post-Victorian Christians of the Church of England variety. They were far from perfect, but good enough. They were honest, hardworking, simple-living, generous folk who believed in their Lord's command to love, serve and give. The first two commandments were the foundation of their lives; *'Love the Lord your God with all your heart, and with all your soul and with all your mind and with all your strength,'* and *'Love your neighbour as yourself' (Bible: Matthew 22:38).* Mum and dad believed this, lived it to the best of their abilities, and taught us five kids to do the same.

From mid-childhood I would always attend 7.30 am worship with dad on a Sunday. I think it was more to do with wanting to be with my dad than any real care about God. Sure I said the words, sang the liturgy and hymns—I enjoyed singing even then—but I didn't have much idea of what it was all about. I did, however, somehow acquire a formidable conscience that caused me great grief because I had a penchant for any mischief I could find. But dad's and mum's teaching and guidance, and dad's beltings when I was too wilful or rebellious—and that was frequently—set me on the path to God and Life, and it's that path I will always be still finding, and trying to point to and encourage here.

Why *'Travel far and wide, tell them why I died'*? And we need to remember that it's not just *tell* but *show* and *tell*. Simply, if we don't embrace for ourselves the life and inner resources taught and demonstrated by the historical Jesus of Nazareth, what we may think of as a good life is really only illusion; a time-limited, predominantly external, material-focussed sequence of events in space. We miss the richness of wonder, of mystery, of being in Love, unlimited in time and space.

In addition, humanity and life as we know it will struggle to survive. Already in the pollution of air, soil and water, in the profligate exploitation and squandering of the finite material resources, in our greed and refusal to share equitably, and in the dramatic changes to climate and eco systems, planet earth is showing signs of great distress.

This Jesus said important things. Scripture reports him as saying *"I am the Way, the Truth and the Life"(Bible: John 14:6)*. This remarkable statement is well discussed in other places and this isn't the place to attempt that again. Let me just say a couple of words about our need to grasp—or, as I've said elsewhere, be grasped by—the essence of this statement. Because, unless we make this essential connection with the mysterious reality to which Christ points, nothing else we do in life will be of any value. It's like installing a solid foundation for a building before any other construction of the building will be secure.

The "Way" refers to many things. Jesus was the bearer, revealer and provider to us of authentic spiritual power enabling us to be truly human. This is our single greatest need in order to have the kind of life that was intended for us. Without this nourishment, all we have is breath and activity; death warmed up, if you like. It's interesting that, at this time in our history, we are increasingly living in world of 'virtual reality'. Our computer games and cyber-space activities are a material metaphor of the kind of existence we have, seem to prefer, and wrongly assume, in our sophisticated foolishness, to be reality. And the vast majority of our life is external to us. Jesus, the 'Way,' is the internal energy—the animating principle—of Love, Spirit, wisdom, release from all ties. This 'unseen' is Reality. This aspect of his being the Way is, arguably, the first and most important.

Together with this 'inner Way' come the other aspects of what Jesus said and did to be the Way. In his physical person he showed and taught us how to be, how to live, how to focus. He showed who we are, what we are worth, what to avoid, and that we are dearly loved. Jesus talked about the correct values for life: love unreservedly and impartially; give generously and joyfully to all without discrimination; serve selflessly in ways that cost us personally. In loving, giving and serving we experience pain together with the joy of both inwardly knowing that we are living well, and of experiencing the responses of those who receive from us. We don't take these actions in order to feel pain or joy; we take them because they are the actions that make life possible and beautiful. To not love, give and serve is to choke life in ourselves and others until it eventually dies. Humanity is at great risk of such a death. We are living as if *we* are the way, the truth and the life. Clearly, we've got something radically wrong. Our way is complex, full of fear, alienating, crushingly heavy on the majority and deceptively light on the few deluded souls doing the crushing. These include captains of industry, politics and all who, unaware of the fear that drives and torments them, seek power over another. The truth is they're seeking power within themselves because, at some deep level beyond their consciousness, they somehow know they have none and are desperately afraid. In contrast, the Christ-follower has none and doesn't care.

Our 'truth' is often rhetoric, manipulation, partial truth, deliberate deception, anything we can get away with; me first. Our life is physical and distorted spiritual; superficial beauty, cleverness, sporting or some other kind of fame, wealth acquisition, shallow and narrow, trinkets and junk. We so-called' developed' nations (a euphemism for the illusion of success) are drowning in stuff; goods and chattels, 'trappings' (often spoken without awareness but accurately describing our fate). More than two billion of our brothers and sisters don't even have clean water to drink. Our way of living is death to millions of our human brothers and sisters, and to countless other life forms. If we don't wake up soon, it may well be death to us all and to most existing life on earth.

At even a superficial glance, we can easily see that the Way Jesus described works. The way we are going doesn't. His Way is peace; our way is war. His Way is love; our way is fear. His Way is joy; our way is sorrow. His way is equality, our way is hierarchy. His Way is release; our way is imprisonment of one kind or another. But why Jesus? Why can't we just see the error of our ways, change, and solve our problems? Probably the short answer is that we've tried for thousands of years and have been steadily and rapidly destroying the planet and ourselves. The self I'm talking about is our lower, 'ego' self outlined in the introduction of this book.

The fact is that no-one gets off this planet alive. Physical death comes to us all. But somewhere deep in our Centre, we know that the True Self is not meant for death; somewhere within ourselves we know that we have an eternal existence beyond the physical; a resurrection life. But, because we have become separated from that True Self, our only remaining experience is the transient nature of what we call life. Why Jesus? Why *travel far and wide and tell them why I died*? Because Jesus somehow mysteriously had within himself the fullness of Life. And this historical Jesus was and is the physical manifestation of this transcendent Spirit Mystery we in the west call God.

We need to again become comfortable talking about God. In ancient cultures, many present-day indigenous cultures and, to a lesser extent amongst other peoples who think of themselves as 'believers', talk of God and the Spirit world is easily and importantly blended with day to day living. This is generally not in many so-called developed nations for a variety of reasons. Whether it be the English 'reserve', the 'private faith' idea, intellectual sophistication or plain arrogance of believing the lie that there is no power higher than us, we have put something between ourselves and God. In that, our submission is inadequate. We have created any number of other 'gods' and give our allegiance and our 'worth-ship' to them; wealth, military might, sex, personal security, etc. And look at the mess we've created. We can send a man to the moon, but we can't live peacefully on earth.

We can talk to someone on a cell phone on the other side of the world, but we can't communicate with our children and neighbours. We can find our way anywhere on earth using Global Navigation Satellite Systems, but we can't find a way to share our possessions with those in need. We can genetically modify food to produce more, but we can't distribute the good, unmodified food we have with those who are hungry. We can create new organs from fatty body tissue, but we can't manage our appetites so as to keep our original organs in good order. We can build amazing structures into the sky, under the sea, across rivers and gulfs, around the world, but we can't extend a hand of loving friendship to someone of a different colour or belief. We've made a mess that we can't seem to clean it up. Or won't.

And we keep looking primarily to science and technology for solutions to problems that are essentially spiritual in nature. Science and technology—as wonderful and valuable as they are—cannot make a heart love, a hand give, a face smile. Those actions are the province of a force much deeper and stronger than the mind and body. They are the work of the Spirit of God within us.

Because God is in and through and before and beyond all that is, God cannot *not* understand and relate to every human experience. Scriptures tell us that God values union above all else. Look at the central aspect of God's nature from the Christian viewpoint: intimate, harmonious, inner community of Father, Son, and Holy Spirit. In this communion is shown the Love that Scriptures tell us God is. And look at your own inner desires for intimacy, security, warmth and belonging, for love within your own relationships with partner, children, grandchildren, friends, parents, and a deep longing to be in peaceful relationship within yourself. It's not difficult in the light of these personal experiences to understand that we are made in the image of Love.

God cannot *not* love, because God is Love. Jesus lived and taught that reality in all he was, did and said. God wants us to know—to experience—that we are deeply loved as a precious son or daughter; that we belong in the family and are an equally valuable and inseparable part of the whole unit. In the light of what we've heard from others during our lives, we may find this hard to accept. It may be helpful to remember that those others were coming from their own struggles to make sense of their own lives, and their best was just not near enough to God's best to give us the truth about ourselves. Most of us are well meaning but somewhat off track for most of our lives. Perhaps our care-givers just didn't know that love is normal. Perhaps they hadn't experienced being well loved themselves.

If you haven't experienced this love that satisfies the longings of your soul, there are reasons. But those reasons don't change the fact of Love. You may never have experienced falling from a great height. But that doesn't change the truth that the force of gravity is an ever present reality that affects you.

Jesus teaches that fear is the opposite of Love. Accordingly, the New Testament says many times, *'fear not' . . . 'perfect love casts out all fear'* (the Love that is God is perfect Love). He taught that Love is the basis of life. Fear is the absence of Love and the basis of death.

So Jesus' 'Way' of Love and life stands over against our way of fear and death. God says *'this day I place before you life and death, blessings and curses. Now choose life that you and your children may live and love your Lord, listen to his voice and hold fast to him. For the Lord is your life and he will give you many years in the land.'(Bible: Deut.30:19-20)*

Let's have a look at the story in the song.

Early morning light can be deceiving
The rising sun reveals the risen one.
Shadows on the lake, their patterns weaving
Standing by the shore God's only Son . . .

This part of the Great Story begins in the weeks after Jesus death and resurrection. The New Testament records that he appeared to several hundred people after his resurrection. He had already appeared to Mary Magdalene, and to the disciples, and breathed on the disciples and said *'receive the Holy Spirit.' (John 20:22)* He appeared again when Thomas was with them. You may remember that Thomas wasn't with them the first time Jesus appeared to the group, and he said *'unless I see him with my own eyes and put my hand into his side, I will not believe'(John20: 25).*

And afterwards, Jesus appeared again to the disciples by the sea of Tiberius early one morning. Some of them had gone out fishing. They were still mystified, confused and stirred up by the death, resurrection and subsequent appearances by Jesus. They wanted him to be their military rescuer, he was crucified and died, they were devastated, he rose from death, they were afraid, excited, confused—a whole range of feelings raged through them. And, in the early light of this morning, this man called out from the shore, *friends, have you got any fish'?*, they called back 'No', and he said *'throw your net out on the other side and you will find some',* and they caught so many fish they couldn't pull them all in. At that moment John realized *'it's the Lord'.*

Every eye is staring at the shoreline
'The Lord is here', the whisper goes around.
They come ashore, eat fish and bread together
And Jesus says to Peter, 'Hear me now' . . .

Now here are some miraculous happenings. A man, Jesus of history, has been nailed to a wooden cross, bled and died, been buried for 2 days, came back to life, appeared to several hundred people, spoke with them, and here he was eating fish and bread with them on the shore of the sea as he had done many times in the previous three years or so. Not only that, but he restored Peter to relationship with himself. You may remember that three times Peter denied knowing Jesus (see Matthew 26: 69-74 for the story) That morning on the shore Jesus asked Peter three times, *'Peter, do you love me'?*

> *'Peter feed my sheep, Peter don't be weak*
> *Follow me wherever that road may lead*
> *Peter do you love me, and nothing else above me*
> *If you do then feed my sheep'*

These words to Peter are now words to you and me if we hear God speaking to us and respond by committing ourselves to follow the Way of Jesus. He says to me, John, do you love me'? He says to you, *(your name)* 'do you love me'? And Jesus isn't talking about a love of sentimentality and emotion—although there may well be some passion! He is talking about who and what he represents. He is one with God. *'I and the Father are one'. (John 10:30, John 14:11) 'If you know me, you know God') John14:7)* Jesus is telling Peter and you and me to seek Love that is Life. That's who Jesus is and represents; that's who God is.

> *The time has come when Jesus must be leaving*
> *He tells them of the Holy One to come*
> *A gift of love to all of his disciples*
> *To give them strength to do what must be done.*

Jesus time and task on earth had finished and he wasn't to remain here any longer. Imagine yourself there on the beach in that early morning light with Jesus, the one who had been your friend, your hero, your teacher, your hope. The one who had celebrated with friends at a wedding, and who had turned water into very good wine so the party could go on. The one who healed the crippled, restored sight to the blind, raised the dead to life. Imagine yourself hearing him speaking to you. *'Friend, I can't stay with you any longer. If I stay with you bodily, the Spirit that really gives the life I've been talking about won't come. But, if I go, I'll send him to you. If you love me you'll do what I say. I'll ask my father and he will give you another Counsellor to be with you forever—the Spirit of Truth.* See John 14-17 for a beautiful summary of who and how we are to be in this life.

Why *'travel far and wide, tell them why I died'*? Because the earth and the lives of every creature in it are being broken and laid waste for lack of knowing and living by Love given to us; love to be received and given on. Luke puts Jesus' final words like this: *'wait for the gift my father promised . . . John baptised with water but in a few days you will be baptised with the Holy Spirit . . . and you will receive power to be my witnesses in Jerusalem, Judea, Samaria and to the ends of the earth'* (Acts 1: 5-8)

What does this mean for us? I think it means that there are no options for life. There is either Truth or absence of Truth. There is either Life or absence of Life. There is only one source of Life. We either willingly choose to cooperate with that Source and become fully human, fully alive and part of life's solution, or we remain less than human, broken and in pain, outside of life and part of the problem. I encourage you to choose life. Then you, too, will want to *'travel far and wide, tell them why (he) died'.*

Chapter Seven

Image of You (Song for Stephanie)

I see you in the first light of day

You shape clouds and paint them to bring me joy

I see you in the freshness around me

And I see you in this child, I see you in this child

No words can say all you are

No music can tell all you do

No picture can show any part of your glory

But this child is the image of you. (Stephanie is the image of you)

I hear you in the wind moving as you will

No leaf remains still you brush every one

I hear you in the creatures near to me

And I hear you in this child, I hear you in this child

I feel you in the stillness of night

Your darkness comes softly and gently holds me

I feel you always warm here beside me

And I feel you in this child, I feel you in this child

Copyright: John White 1983

Ray and Sheila Dallin have been friends of ours for many years. They had three fine and much loved boys (and still do), Chip, Corey and Ben. Then Stephanie was born—the first and much loved daughter. As was the tradition at our little church family—a quite unusual for-the-time Anglican house church of about a hundred—I often wrote songs for special occasions. As was also the tradition for many of the families, rather than baptising infants, we often had a celebration of their birth and 'dedicated' them to God's care. The dedication left the celebration of baptism to the discretion of the child as they grew old enough to know what it was about and to choose for themselves.

These dedications, like all our gatherings, were wonderful, joyful, noisy occasions which included all family members. We had babies crawling around the floor, toddlers tripping over everyone as they wobbled through the crowd sitting on cushions on the floor, young parents, singles and oldies all in together. One of the great qualities of this little community was that there was a sense of belonging as one family. This experience was transformational for everyone. In a time when dislocation and alienation of the individual was accelerating, here was a small island of belonging in a community committed to and transforming in the Love of God. Thirty years later, our now adult children still recall the benefits of having many sets of parents with any of whom they would happily go for a night or longer as required. I recall a time when our son, Ben, who was about 23 at the time had a sporting incident in which he sustained a heavy contact with another player. His chest was compressed and he was in pain. His first thought was 'call Joan'! Joan Jessup was a member of our home group, a senior nurse and, as far as Ben was concerned, the authority on matters medical! Joan was a second mum to both Ben and Emma. My wife, Jennifer, and I enjoyed playing roles in amateur musicals for many years. When things got a bit torrid at home, and the kids were tired of mum and dad disciplining them for one thing or another, Emma and Ben were noted as saying 'why don't you and mum do another musical so we can stay with Joan and Michael'? We were blessed to be part of this extended family. And it's good to remember that a functional community is an image of God. But I digress again.

This occasion was the dedication of Stephanie, and Ray and Sheila asked me some months prior if I would write a song for Stephanie's dedication. There was no question. Of course I would. It would be an honour to write a song for such a special occasion. We left it at that. For weeks I had no idea what to write. Then, one night while I was contemplating this dilemma, I got a single thought, 'God, this child is the image of you'. That was it. Then, as is often the case either through my personal lack of discipline, absence of inspiration, or both, the night before the celebration was the time when the rest of the song came. And it came to me that we see and experience the mystery of the Divine Presence as much in the natural order as in any specific spiritual event. I was raised in the bush in the south-west of Western Australia in the small town of Mt Barker. The wonders of huge eucalypt trees, kangaroos, rabbits, magpies, Wedge-Tailed Eagles, all manner of other creatures, hills and creeks, electrical storms, clouds tinted by early morning light and the soft darkness of days end were my place of being. I felt more peaceful and connected to life while I was walking or working outdoors than anywhere else; I felt God more in the natural order than in any church building or service. I suspect that is true for many. And I also knew, at least in my mind at that time that, somehow the nature of God was infused into the human being in a very special, mysterious way that made us after the likeness of God. I didn't know what that really meant and still don't. But I do know that God is sufficiently knowable for us to seek, and with whom to settle into union; a union that is a mystical knowing far beyond our mental abilities.

So as I sat to write the song for Stephanie, the images and experiences of my encounter with the wonder of life came to me in yet another beautiful child, Stephanie, the newest, wonderful mystery of being. This is really a conversation with God about the wonder of creation and, in particular, this child Stephanie Dallin. It's also a song about you and me. You are this child. I am this child.

'I see you in the first light of day,
you shape clouds and paint them to bring me joy,
I see you in the freshness around me,
and I see you in this child; I see you in this child'.

Have you noticed how fresh and new everything feels in the early morning? If not, get up earlier than you need to tomorrow, and experience it. I know it can be great to linger those extra few minutes in a warm bed. But there's something more resting and reinvigorating to just be up in the first light of day. The events of yesterday and the night have passed, the earth is cooler, the air is usually heavier and cleaner. Perhaps there's dew, frost or snow underfoot. If there's dust, even that seems to stay on the ground because of a little more dampness. If you're early enough, there are no birds stirring yet. There are few people and things moving. There's a sense of stillness even if there's a strong wind blowing where you are. The stillness is in you. Somehow in this gift to you of a fresh, new day, there is a newness to life. If you choose to allow yourself to be aware of this, you can't help but see it and sense it. And awareness is the key. Much of life just passes us by in a tumultuous rush and we don't even notice it. But as we choose to tune in to what's around and within us, a fresh experience comes to us. We are 'being'. We're not doing and rushing. Just being. And, no matter what our circumstances, this 'being' can be full of wonder; full of delight. Some guru once said, *'don't just do something; sit there!* There's great wisdom in that.

As we stop, we experience the simple gifts that come continuously with every new day and night, every encounter with the physical universe, and with every breath. As we become still, we 'see' in a new way—both with new physical eyes, and with deeper eyes of the soul. It is as if we wake up from a sort of half-sleep in which we move around but are not really awake. If someone asked you what you saw on the way to work, you probably wouldn't be able to tell them more than a tiny fraction of what you passed. While that is normal, it is an abnormal normal; it's not being fully alive. If someone asked you what you saw in Helen this morning, you might say 'she was wearing a red dress and there was something different about her hair'. Did you see the intricacy of her eyes, the tone or texture of her skin, the expression that gave a hint of her feeling sad or uncomfortable? Did you see into her soul, her centre? Did you relate to anything of her humanity? Did she seem somehow like you? When we wake up, we begin to see the reality of the depth of life rather than just the superficialities. We begin to see ourselves more similar to others than different from them. We see that we are each a fragment of the great oneness that is life.

I hear you in the wind moving as you will,
No leaf remains still, you brush every one
I hear you in the creatures near to me,
And I hear you in this child; I hear you in this child

In Hebrew and some other languages, there is one word for spirit, wind and breath. No-one knows from where the wind comes or to where it goes. Sure, meteorologists can measure and tell us about pressure systems and general patterns of circulation, and can predict roughly the direction, temperature, humidity and strength of winds. And although we have some notion of a certain wind, there are frequently gusts, lulls and shifts both subtle and dramatic in every dimension of this mysterious and unseen flow of air across the surface of this amazing planet. We see it and hear it by it's effect on water, dust and vegetation and other physical surfaces, but we don't see the wind. It blows where it will. It has an energy and life of its own. In a similar way, our breath is somehow the energy for our life. We don't really understand it. We don't think about it. It just happens automatically for most of us for all the days of our lives. It is part of the mystery of life.

As we acknowledge and tune into this mystery, we become empowered by this great energy that produces and sustains all life; a mysterious stream flowing within and through and from all human beings who seek it. In such people we experience a depth of being far beyond the senses, mind or reason. There is a profound thankfulness for, and acceptance and willing embrace of, this gift that comes without any ability on our part. We simply receive. For many, there may be no conscious acknowledgment of this great mystery. For those who choose to cooperate with life and seek it in all its fullness, there is a much deeper engagement with and experience of life. And, in them, there is generally a powerful, loving, gentleness and generosity towards all life that is an integral part of the creative processes of life in the universe. This love-powered way of being is such that there are no words to adequately express it. Like the wind or the breath, we hear it come and go and all we can do is be in it and with it, for we are part of it and it is part of us.

No words can say all you are
No music can tell all you do
No picture can show any part of your glory
But this child is the image of you; this child is the image of you

Words can't describe the creator of the universe. The best we can do is tentatively express directions towards that great Reality. If anyone says they can describe God to you, don't listen to them. They don't know God. They only know their personal projections of what they think God is; their descriptions will always be inadequate. Their ideas and words are between them and God, and will most likely get between you and God. Thoughts and words become barriers. If our goal is to continue towards God, to have anything—even profound thoughts—between us and our goal is to deny our attainment of that goal. If God is infinite, how can that infinite be described by the finite; a mere creature?

There is a saying from one of the wisdom traditions: *'the one who speaks, doesn't know; the one who knows, doesn't speak'*. Although well-meaning—and I think most human beings are, by nature, well-meaning—to be adamant about the infinite seems a little arrogant. It may be wiser to be tentative in our understanding. Such an attitude tends to open reality to us far more effectively than anything we can do to engage it, and opens us to one another. It is written elsewhere, *'no eye has seen, nor ear heard, nor mind conceived what God has prepared for those who love him"* (Bible: 1Corinthians, 2:9). So, it seems good to acknowledge that God is able to do whatever is necessary for us, and we don't need to concern ourselves much at all about those abilities.

'No music can tell all you do'. One of the universal languages of humanity is music. When words make no sense to our minds, the pitch of notes, tones, rhythms, combination of instruments, sounds, timbre, volume, expression—all that makes up this experience we call music—seem to speak to us all at a level deeper than our minds. Music engages the soul and spirit, the emotions, the hopes, dreams, disappointments—everything that is or has been or promises to be our lives. And yet, as wonderful and moving as music can be it, too, cannot be fully comprehended as to its union with the hearer, writer or player. Like

the spirit, there is something mystical about music; something beyond the gross senses that apprehend it only in part. Music is both a gift to us and something we can create. As such, it has both a mysteriously indescribable quality—and, thus, transcends us—and it is the product of our finiteness so it can never tell all that there is in the great Realty of life.

To spend much time dissecting music, analysing, evaluating its merits, thinking and talking about it, is of little value to us. It could be likened to placing a great value on being able to describe the flavour of some delicious meal. Far better for your body, mind and soul to simply enjoy the experience of the meal. Or talking about a fabulous opera or other musical performance. Much more satisfying to be there allowing each sound, each vibration to wash over and through you and transport you beyond your mind and body to another dimension of being. The grave danger of the mental practices of analysing, is that we allow ourselves to be distracted from our being. A wise teacher once said to me 'don't follow the mind; it'll take you down a dark alley and mug you'. In this he echoes the wise women and men throughout history who recognized the diabolical (I choose the word carefully) connection between thoughts and feeling states. Thoughts that produce a negative emotional reaction obviously detract from quality of life. Thoughts that produce a positive emotional response—although generally much better for us—can also be dangerous in that we may come to depend on them to make us feel OK.

No-one is capable of thinking good thoughts all the time. Therefore, following the mind will result in a roller-coaster experience of life. The thinker will remain attached to the process of thoughts creating feelings. While s/he is attached to any such process, s/he cannot move beyond the sense-mind-reason continuum to experience union with Truth, which is beyond the reach of these abilities

The well being of the True Self is not reliant upon good thoughts that produce good feelings, nor is it disturbed by 'bad thoughts' producing 'bad feelings'.

The experience of music is not primarily in the words, but in the notes. Profound words with a weak score will not move a listener as much as ordinary words with a powerful musical score. The magic is in the dots, the pauses between them, and how they are performed. Something in our Centre knows how to connect with music.

No picture can show any part of your glory. Rather than labour the points mentioned above, an image—a photograph or an artist's representation, no matter how beautiful or skilful—generally does not produce the same experience in a viewer as being with or in the scene being represented. Again it's to do with the finite attempting to represent the infinite. Of course, it is absolutely valid for an artist to produce his or her subjective experience of a given object, and such expressions have great value as part of the one by whom they were produced, and also as providers of pleasure for those viewing the work. Whatever expression the artist may choose to represent his or her subject, the experience, for example, of humidity, temperature, aroma or movement of air around the subject cannot be represented truly.

But this child is the image of you (God!)

How can we talk about this in words that are not religious jargon yet can at least point towards the Realty to which they allude? This is one of the great challenges of the wisdom traditions in humankind—and, especially the religious communities. We need to become increasingly aware of and at home with our own 'being in God', so that this central fact of life is naturally and easily present in all we are and do and say. And in that, we need to become sufficiently comfortable with the mystery so that we are not tempted to move ourselves and others into error by being prescriptive.

If God is mystery *"my thoughts are above your thoughts and my ways above your ways', says the Lord (Isaiah 55:9)'We see now in a glass, darkly, but then, face to face' (1 Corinthians 13:12)*and we are created in the image of God, the same mysterious nature is in us. Although we are finite in our creatureliness we are, in some significant ways, reflections of the infiniteness of God. Scripture also says a great deal about God being Love. If God is Love, and God is the architect and builder of the universe, then Love is the creative power somehow responsible for and permeating the universe. And we, too, in our deepest centre are Love.

When I saw our two babies, Emma and Benjamin, or little Stephanie or, more recently, our first two grandsons, Hamish and Nathan, it is easy to see, hear and feel the beauty, the delicacy, the miracle of love in these tiny beings. Created by the power of transcendent love in and through the unitive love of their parents, these little creatures are created 'after the likeness of and in the image of God (Genesis 1: 26) who is Love (1 John 4: 16). *This child is the image of you.* You are the child. I am the child. We each bear the stamp of the nature of the creative power upholding and sustaining the universe.

Although God is beyond our mind's ability to comprehend, God can be sufficiently experienced and, thus, known. Perhaps it is more correct to say that we can be known by God, because we don't have what it takes to do the connecting. But, as has been said earlier, it is a mystical knowing—an intuitive knowing; a knowing from within you and within me. As has been expressed by mystics such as St John of the Cross it is a knowing without knowing, knowing through loving, knowing through being immersed in and being one with God.

Because much of our connection with the mystery of God is through the external physical world of the senses, it can also be experienced as

'*I feel you in the stillness of night, your darkness comes softly and gently holds me, I feel you always warm here beside me, and I feel you in this child; I feel you in this child'.*

We must learn to enter the stillness and silence within ourselves—quieten our restless and noisy minds and bodies in order to experience the still, small voice of God at the centre of the soul. There is a soft, strong, secure experience in this inner knowing. It has the sense of the comfort of warmth around you. This has been my experience and was when the words of the song came to me in that night before the dedication of Stephanie Dallin.

. . . .

Chapter Eight

I Was Hungry

The King will say to those at his right hand
Come, oh come, oh blessed of my father
Inherit the kingdom prepared for you
I was hungry and you gave me food
I was thirsty and you brought a drink to me
I was a stranger and you welcomed me
I was naked and you clothed me
Sick and you visited me, in prison and you came to me
And the righteous will answer him, the righteous will answer him

Lord when did we see you hungry and feed you or thirsty and give you
a drink
And when did we see you a stranger and welcome you, or naked and
clothe you,
And when did we see you sick or in prison, Lord, and visit you
And the king will answer them, 'truly I say to you
As you did it once for the least of mine, you did it for me'

Then he will say to those at his left hand
'Depart from me, depart from me, I never knew you

Eternal fire, oh cursed, is for you.

I was hungry and you gave me no food

I was thirsty and you gave no drink to me

I was a stranger you didn't welcome me,

I was naked you didn't clothe me

Sick you didn't visit me

In prison and you stayed away

And they will answer him, they will answer him . . .

Lord when did we see you hungry or thirsty

Lord when did we see you a stranger or naked

Lord when did we see you sick or in prison, and minister not to you.

And he will answer them,' truly I say to you

As you did it not to the least of mine, you did it not to me'

It could be argued that humanity is unravelling. It's so cliché that I wince to say it, but the gap between those who have and those who have not is more like a chasm and still widening; a pain-filled, gaping void of both despair and shame. At one extreme, great suffering and despair for millions for whom survival is a daily struggle. At the other, the decreasing few for whom the ride is ever more pleasure-laden and who should, but don't, experience the shame of their (our) 'theft'. For some of us, of course, it is not theft, because we suffer from the most insidious disease of all—unawareness; we don't know what we are doing. For others, even more pitiable, it is theft, because we know what we're doing but don't care. For us, it's all here for the taking. If we're smart enough, lucky enough, business-like enough (a euphemism for callous and inhuman), it's our right. The former group may be thought of as ignorant, and pitiable; the latter may well be evil. I hesitate to even suggest such a heavy thought, but it's one that needs to be considered in this age in which the phrase 'dog eat dog' is a kindergarten version of what's actually happening.

Some of our brothers and sisters are rationalising and justifying every evil there is in the name of 'the market economy, growth, national security, democracy' or any number of other euphemistic obscenities that characterize our modern, western vernacular. We are extremely skilled at creating and using words to distance ourselves from the reality of our disgraceful, inhuman actions. A couple worth noting here are 'pre-emptive strike'—an obscene denial of the reality more accurately named *'cold-bloodedly waging war by unprovoked attacking and slaughtering of tens of thousands of women, children, and other non-combatants, and the wholesale destruction of essential human services infrastructure of a sovereign nation'*. A second is 'rendition'. This obscenity is better called *'kidnapping, torture, detaining without charge or evidence, trashing human hearts, minds, souls and bodies of all involved'* and, if that's not disgraceful enough, doing it all in the name of democracy and even God. That kind of democracy we don't need in this world. And God is in the business of giving life, not taking it.

Unless we wake up and see what we're doing, and how far removed it is from the way that living together on this planet is actually workable, we are in deep trouble, and so is life as we know it on planet earth. And I'm an optimist. I'm ever hopeful that we will rise to our glorious potential as lovers of all creation; as co-creators with the architect of the universe and, as a group, make changes that will acknowledge our errors, and display our glorious Essence.

Someone once asked Thomas a'Kempis *'don't you despair at the condition of mankind?'* The wise Thomas responded, *'knowing the darkness of the human heart I'm surprised there's not more evil in the world'* (Of the Imitation of Christ). Someone else said, *'for evil to flourish, all that is necessary is for good people to do nothing'*. One group that has accepted this truth and decided to work it in the positive, is World Vision—one of the great humanitarian organizations of this present age. One of the projects started by World Vision many years ago was the '40-Hour Famine'—an invitation for us westerners—the 'haves'—to volunteer to go without food for a period of just 40 hours and, through hourly sponsorship, also raise funds for this great human work of justice, mercy and compassion.

As I recall, it was in 1980 that I was the Youth Education Officer at Kelmscott Senior High School in Perth, Western Australia, at the time when the 40-Hour Famine came around. I was one of the teacher-coordinators of the ISCF (Inter-School Christian Fellowship). My colleague, Dr Mark Williams, was another, and the Newhouse kids and their wonderful parents, Mavis and Chris were passionate supporters of this movement of compassion and life for all. I apologise to all those others who were involved whose names I cannot recall, (you know who you are) but who are as precious as any human being who has ever walked the earth. Thank you for struggling to find and be the truth in life at that time!

I remember we spent the weekend of the 40-Hour Famine together in the school drama room. We ate nothing but the occasional barley-sugar and we drank nothing but water and a little fruit juice. And we were fortunate to have that! Our stomachs grumbled a bit but it wasn't the real deprivation known by so many others. As I write this, there are more than two billion people who don't have clean drinking water. That is our shame and one of our challenges. As we spent the weekend together uncomfortably aware of our seldom-challenged stomachs, we discussed and read from Scriptures about the whole poverty-starvation situation in our world. The bible passage on which we focussed for the weekend was from the gospel of Matthew, chapter 25 verses 34 to 45. As we spent the 40 hours doing whatever we could to keep our minds off our pathetically groaning stomachs (we didn't know what it was like to be even a little hungry, really), we played games, read, talked about the condition of humanity and our part in it, etc, and I was inspired to write the song, *'I Was Hungry'*.

If you are of another religious persuasion, I'm confident you'll forgive me for quoting from the Christian Scriptures from which the lyrics were almost literally lifted. If you are from no particular religious persuasion, just allow the words of justice, mercy and compassion to speak to you.

I don't know what benefits flowed from that weekend for others who were there. I do know that I created a song from words of universal wisdom that have had a great effect on me and on many who have heard it since. I reflected, for the first time, that I am involved with the suffering of all other human beings. As I read and re-read those words *'I was hungry and you gave me no food'*, I became aware that I was the one being talked about as the withholder. I had food. Millions of others had none. I was responsible to share what I had with as many as I could. How I lived had an effect on every other human being. As John Donne said so eloquently in his 17th meditation, *'No man is an island entire of itself, but each is a part of the maine; if a clod bee washed away, England is the lesse; as if thy manor were, or the manor of thy friend were. Each man's death diminishes me, for I am involved in mankind . . . therefore do not send to know for whom the bell tolls: it tolls for thee.'* I came to know that weekend, that everything I do has an effect on everyone and everything else in all creation. If I have more than I need, someone else is likely to have less than they need. I still live far out of balance and use far more than I need to the detriment of my brothers and sisters who do not even have the necessities that provide dignity. But I am daily aware of the discrepancy and daily attempt to redress the inequity. I read recently that the richest person is not the one who has the most, but the one who needs the least and gives the most.

As you consider the words of this song, I hope you listen with your heart renewed by the deep voice of Love that flows within every human being whether or not they yet know or experience it. I hope you are moved to become even more radically different than you are at present, and thankful to the great Creator of Life for everything. I hope you become aware that 'they' are always 'us'. I hope you become aware that we are inextricably one with each other and with the great Oneness of all that is. I hope you come to deeply know that everything you do or don't do has an impact on every other person and creature in existence. If you weren't aware of just how linked we are, consider this bit of interesting trivia:

> *'Scientists tell us that in your next breath you will breathe in 400,000 of the argon atoms breathed out by Gandhi in his long life. Argon atoms are here from the last supper, the arguments of the diplomats of Yalta, and from the recitations of the classic poets. We have argon from the sighs of ancient lovers, from the battle cries at Waterloo, and even from last years argonic output of . . .* anyone you care to bring to mind, really. *(From Harlow Shapley, Harvard Astronomer, in 'Sacred Balance' David Suzuki)*

We don't live in isolation. We cannot say, it's not my problem. We each share responsibility for everything that happens to every other creature. When we know that and live it, suffering will be dramatically reduced on earth. There are many of us who purport to worship God. But our worship is just noise unless our lives are congruent with our worship. In fact, it could be seen as a bit of a concern that experiences of 'musical worship'—especially in the Christian context—are an increasing focus for young seekers. Our teaching of all our young people needs to ensure that they are aware that words and emotional experiences may be a good start, but only that—a start. We need to demonstrate in our own lives that actions must be congruent with words or the words are meaningless. In fact, they are worse than that because the world is watching. If we don't do what we sing about, not only do observers reject our words, they reject the One who inspires the words. That can lead to their spirits never again being willing to hear the deep, inner calling of Love.

So, the challenge for each of is to reassess our lives and either stop saying 'I believe in so and so', or start demonstrating that belief.

Most spiritual seekers of any persuasion attest to the above suggestion. The growing divisions in humanity support the fact that what we're doing can't be right because it isn't working. Divisions in a world of Oneness are incongruous. Later we'll talk more about arbitrary divisions which are the creation of a mankind in ill-health. If we saw correctly, we would see that we are one family. Our democratic protestations, for example, have no substance because they generate profiteering and power-mongering at the cost to others less powerful, and dramatic inequities wherever so-called democracy exists on the planet.

But let's move on to the key message in the song.

I was hungry and you gave me food
I was thirsty and you brought a drink to me
I was a stranger and you welcomed me
I was naked and you clothed me
Sick and you visited me, in prison and you came to me.

How can it make sense to do anything other than what is suggested in the words above? How can anyone claim some kind of divine right to extra resources simply because an accident of birth placed them in a richly—resourced part of the planet? You need greater faith than I have to believe that anyone has more right than anyone else to the basic requirements for a dignified life. The words of this song are universal wisdom. They place you and me and every other human being on the same worth footing. The Great Provider is stating the reality; all are to be fed, watered, clothed, healed and visited. None are to be cast away as somehow less than the ones who control the systems of the day.

In the work I am currently doing in prisons on a restorative justice model, it is interesting to note that the vast majority of those high up in the system making all the decisions about what happens to prisoners have never even met a prisoner! How could they make informed decisions about what might be beneficial to the healing of these members of our society? The reason many have never met a prisoner is that are afraid. They've got the common, yet false, belief that prisoners are somehow more evil than the rest of us. The irrational fear created by this wrong belief effectively separates us from each other and, as tragically, from ourselves and who we could, and were meant to, become: magnificent, loving, generous, life-giving beings! That's who we really are! We just haven't adequately appropriated it yet.

When we generously give food, drink, clothing, healing and companionship to all who are in need of such, we are in that moment living like royalty, living in the light, peaceful, joyful, bountiful. And we need to remember it is not we who are giving; all we have was given to us. It is not our own cleverness that created the bounty; it is a gift. We are not to treat what we have as ours, but as entrusted to us to use wisely and compassionately for the good of all.

When we give in this way, something mystical happens. In the act of giving, we are transported beyond our (ego) selves into a realm of divinity, for want of a better word; a realm in which for that moment we are detached from all that separates us from our True Selves, from one another, and from all that is. In that moment we are separated from all that puts us under pressure and causes us to suffer. Giving is normal for human beings. Giving is good for *us*. Psychologists tell us that we cannot *not* be self-satisfying. We are giving because it is good for us. The fact that it benefits the other is a wonderful bonus. The act of giving is a divine reality that brings life just because it is right and true.

What does it mean '*when you did it for one of the least of mine, you did it for me*' I think the 'me' being talked about here is God. And so, when you 'do it' (give of yourself), at that moment you are one with the True Self and with God. You are awake. You 'get it' and 'are it' at that moment!

The next bit of the song talks about the reverse. Let's consider that a bit for what it holds for us.

Then he will say to those at his left hand
Depart from me, depart from me, I never knew you
Eternal fire, oh cursed, is for you.
I was hungry and you gave me no food

I was thirsty and you gave no drink to me
I was a stranger you didn't welcome me,
I was naked you didn't clothe me
Sick you didn't visit me
In prison and you stayed away
And they will answer him, they will answer him . . .

Lord when did we see you hungry or thirsty
Lord when did we see you a stranger or naked
Lord when did we see you sick or in prison, and minister not to you.
And he will answer them, truly I say to you
As you did it not to the least of mine, you did it not to me

The central point here is *'I never knew you'*. Put another way, *'we weren't together; you were going your way, it wasn't my way, which is the way that leads to life'*. Our understanding of this line, *'I never knew you'*, is crucial to our wellbeing as individuals, and as the human community. It expresses the truth that those who are not tuned in to the great reality, were never known. Their whole life, they didn't get it. They were and are like the prodigal son who, for a time, was wandering in the wilderness of life having cut himself off from the supports of his family community, the place of his belonging and security and nurture.

Whatever we may believe about the next line, *'eternal fire, oh cursed, is for you'*, our analysing what it might mean would only take our focus from the real matter of concern, and that is where are we in all this? It is easy and safe to focus on anyone or anything other than ourselves. But it is not helpful. On the other hand, the most helpful thing we can do is fearlessly, honestly and continuously choose to concern ourselves only with what we intuit, value, believe, say and do. These actions within us are the only things over which we have any control in this life, and the only things for which we are to be totally responsible. Ourselves. It's not that difficult to understand. It's just difficult to do because it is exceptionally painful to become aware, to feel, and to admit that there is wrong in us. There is darkness in us. There is shame and guilt and fear in us. There is deep dread that we are not all we know we ought to be. And there is healing and wholeness in nothing else than this realization and the resultant, committed action to change ourselves

When someone is hungry and I am able to give them food but fail to do so, I am responsible for their hunger.

When someone is thirsty and I am able to provide them a drink but fail to do so, I am responsible for their thirst.

When anyone on earth lacks the necessities of dignity and I fail to do what I can to reverse that deprivation, I share responsibility for their indignity.

When someone is sick or in prison and I fail to do what I can to ensure they are visited and cared for as people of equal worth to me, I am responsible for their suffering and I am guilty of inhumanity.

In this pivotal statement, the Jesus of history is saying something more central to us than anything else we may choose to consider. He is saying, '*when you do it not to the least of mine, you do it not to me*'. He is giving us a parable—a story that we might relate to—about how we are to live. Here he is saying if we don't care for every other being, we are not living in the Light, in Love. In short, we are kidding ourselves about being 'good people' or 'Christian ' or 'spiritual' or any other righteous label we might fancy using to describe ourselves. We are asleep. We are lost. We are sub-human. Jesus didn't say 'praise me, use my name a lot, say certain words and all will be well'. No. He said love, serve and give. Don't judge, don't analyse, don't condemn. That's not your job. Love, serve, give. Justice, mercy, compassion. That's our job.

So, whatever we may think may be after this life, Jesus is more concerned *with* this life and how well we live it. His instructions, and those of many other teachers through history, are clear. And I can tell how well I am living when someone is hungry and I do everything I can to feed them, thirsty and I do everything I can to give them a drink, naked and I clothe them, sick or in prison and I visit them and show genuine love and responsibility for them. When I live in this way, I am in union with God and all is well.

Chapter Nine

How Full of Wonder

Reflections of your beauty I see
And sounds of your majesty come to me wherever I turn
Even the babbling of babes and the laughter of children
Spell out your name

When I gaze into star-printed skies
The work of your fingers enfolds me, in amazement I stand
For what am I, my master, that you should watch over
And care for me

Wonder, how full of wonder
Splendour, how full of splendour you are

You have crowned me with glory
And made me so like you that you even call me your child
Into my care you gave all the work of your hands,
You gave it to me

Wonder, how full of wonder
Splendour, how full of splendour
Wonder, how full of wonder you are.

I can't say that I have a favourite song. Some people do. Maybe you are one of them. But most people at least have a certain style of song or music that they enjoy; that they identify with for some reason. They may be able to tell you what the connection is; they may not. They may have different styles of music depending on either the mood they are in, or the mood they would like to be in. At Christmas 2007, our daughter, Emma, gave me a book titled 'Musicophilia'. One of the themes of the book is the human being's inherent predisposition for creating and listening to music. It seems that we are hard wired for music in ways of which we are not even aware. Many stories are presented of amazing musical experiences and abilities manifesting in people who have suffered some kind of trauma or near death experience. Our connection with music seems to be as profound as it is mysterious. And we may think we are choosing the music. But it may be more the case that music chooses us for what we need from it.

David was kind of a song-writer. He wasn't an ordinary bloke. He was King of Israel. In the middle of the Bible, is the book of Psalms. There are one hundred and fifty of them. 'Psalm' is another word for song or hymn—an expression with or without music of the deepest part of the human soul and spirit. They were written between two and a half and three and a half thousand years ago. About half were written by King David.

At times of trouble in life, many people who don't usually read the Bible at all will most often turn to the Psalms. The most widely known is Psalm twenty three: *'The Lord is my shepherd, I shall not want. He makes me lie down in green pastures, he leads me beside still waters, he restores my soul . . . '* These great words of comfort seem to have a magical pull and effect on anyone who is in trouble of any kind. Comfort in times of trouble is one of the great themes of this collection of writings. But we don't have to be in trouble to draw great benefit from the Psalms. These writings have something for every human experience.

They help us to meet God intimately, to learn about and understand more of God and ourselves, to feel a sense of belonging to the one great human family which has only one Father/Mother (we are all brothers and sisters). Although there is a fair bit of horrible stuff in the Psalms—much like life as we know it—many of them help us to know we are provided for, safe, valued and loved, and we have a reason for being here that is bigger than ourselves. They help us to be thankful, to find contentment in any circumstance, to celebrate life, to praise and worship God, to care for each other and for our planet, and to know there is nothing that can separate us from God and true well-being. Many psalms remind us that no matter what is happening, all is well. There is nothing to fear if we acknowledge that we belong to and in and with God and each other. Fear is only a reality if we choose to turn our back on that belonging.

In the world around us we see great distress and destruction. The root cause of this distress is our failure to put adequate constraints on the ego—the wilful, individual small self—and to understand who we really are and how this whole thing called creation and life actually works. We are the only creatures on the planet who produce waste. We are the only creatures who are systematically destroying the habitat that sustains us. It could be argued that apes and elephants do also. But their destruction is mainly due to the tiny remnant of habitat that we humans have left them. Our actions are driven by greed, which has its roots in fear and lack of awareness of Reality. We can guarantee nothing in this life other than no-one gets off the planet alive. And let's not forget taxes! We need to find within ourselves the ability to trust that all will somehow be OK. Each breath is given to us. We can't prolong our days. All we can do is graciously accept each breath and each provision as it comes to us, and acknowledge the reality that it is given by someone far greater than us. Then we can begin to live well, content with enough for now, not worrying about storing up great amounts of provision of any sort, but treading lightly on the earth and being generous so that all have sufficient. And as we trust that that is this right way to be, provision for all creatures will continue as we need, although not necessarily as we might want.

A little later, we'll talk more about wanting; the reasons for it and the destruction it causes to us and to all others. But, for now, let's continue to focus on what we can do to ensure as far as possible that all goes well with us. And what we can do—and must do—is realize that we can't create and sustain life in our own strength and abilities. That is the province of the one we might call God; the One who alone is responsible for the wonder, the mystery of all that is, and who invites us as both guests and co-creators to enjoy and care for the life we have been given.

One little Psalm that speaks of both the wonder of God and the invitation for us to be partners, is Psalm 8.

This was one of the Bible readings set down for a particular week at our church and, as was normal practice in those days, I would try to write a song specifically for the day to reinforce the words of Scripture and the teaching. As I reflected on the words, I was drawn to spend some time outside. I lived in the city of Perth at the time, but we still had a good clear view of the big night sky with the magnificent Milky Way of the Southern Hemisphere. So I spent time lying on my back on some grass looking up at the stars and just being amazed over and over again. We were close enough to the ocean to feel the cool sea breeze at the end of that hot day. Our suburb was quite leafy and open. We are amongst the most fortunate people in the world to be able to live in such surroundings; so many others have so much less it doesn't seem just at all. Birds and insects and other little creatures were going about their busy lives. And there were people of various ages out for a stroll. Because we were at that stage in life and ours was a new suburb, there were lots of children around us in our community.

As I thought about the words of Psalm 8, and on all that surrounded me, I was filled again with a sense of humility and awe at just how amazing this life and universe is. This little song was a gift of my amazement.

It is said in scripture, *'Where can I flee from your presence? If I go up to heaven, you are there; if I make my bed in the depths, you are there . . .* (Psalm 139:7-10).

If God created all things, God's presence is somehow in all things. Again, Scripture says *'in him we live and move and have our being (Bible: Acts. 17:28).* This is saying not only that God is in us, but that we are in God. Our life and the life of all things is contained in God. There is nothing and nowhere we can be where this creative presence of God is not. Every part of creation reflects the creative presence of God. Lakes, rivers, forests, mountains, deserts, decaying bones, air, fire, all creatures. We cannot go or look anywhere and not see God, because God's presence permeates every particle of matter. Even though so much of our surroundings may seem to be oppressive and filled with death and suffering, somehow if we look deeply, we will see God. We must. If we only see the pain, the struggle, the brokenness, we will despair and be living a death. Scripture's promise is that God is everywhere and that God *'works all things together for good for those who love him, who are called according to his purposes'(Rom: 8:28)* This seems to be saying that anything—pleasant or unpleasant to us—can be used for our good if we are willing to open ourselves to that idea and accept that promise as good.

Of course much of the pain we feel and the destruction we see around us, we cause for ourselves by our rejection of God. Even so, we are seeing God; God is even in our rejection of God. If you can do nothing but breathe this breath, be aware that God is present in that breath and somehow, all is well. To not be able to do so, is to be overwhelmed by external circumstance, much of which is created by us. Although we humans are a natural part of the created order, when we act without reference to God, we remove ourselves from the divine presence and, so, we suffer and cause suffering. When we fail to live with care for the whole of life, that failure is because we have not been effectively taught and we don't practice knowing who we really are and what we are really to be about.

Reflections of your beauty I see,

If we look with the eyes of our hearts—our True eyes—we will see the wonder of the Great Reality that we may call God wherever we look. To not choose to see in this way is to choose to die before we stop breathing. That is a great tragedy of this present age. We see mostly with physical eyes, and with motives that serve only ourselves and, perhaps, a few others close to us. Look at a leaf; even a decaying leaf. Become aware of the intricate design and construction of this amazing 'energy factory' and it's effect on you and other creatures. Think about how it is nourished by nutrients and water taken up from the earth by the roots of the tree of which it is part. Think about how it develops from a tiny bud, itself the product of an amazing DNA programme. Think about how its elements interact with sunlight to produce nourishment for both the tree and creatures who are served by it. And think about the way it takes substances from the atmosphere that are poisonous to humans and all manner of creatures, transforms and stores them in it's substance, and returns life-giving oxygen to that atmosphere, and water vapour to moisten the air and eventually develop into rain to refresh the earth and sustain the great cycles of life. To not be left in absolute wonder by such processes is to be far removed from our roots as integral parts of this great Whole. And that's just a leaf! What awe could be inspired by the great mountains continually being forced up by the immense pressures produced by great underground plates of the earth's crust colliding. Or by other mountains that have been formed over billions of years through erosion by wind and water and heat.

And sounds of your majesty come to me wherever I turn'

Where I live, we have a bird called the Magpie. It is a medium sized bird, vivid white on black, and lives in colonies each with their own territory. Apart from its beauty, it has one of the most beautiful songs of any bird I have ever heard. If I could only pick one bird-song to hear forever, it would be the song of the West Australian Magpie. As it is impossible to describe God, it is impossible to describe the song of the Magpie. That makes sense when we consider that God's creative, indescribable presence is in the magpie. Like many birds, the Magpie has a repertoire of sounds for various occasions. And they vary in intensity, volume, tone, cadence, and so on. When danger approaches, there is a piercing, urgent, loud cry, which is very different from it's contented, community singing. These *sounds of majesty* are, for me, most beautiful and peacefully haunting on a clear, cold night when the moon is full and I'm outside my home (which is surrounded by bush). I don't know how they get up for breakfast in the morning, because sometimes they carol and warble all night. I hear one colony singing nearby, then they quieten for a while and another colony starts up as if in reply. This 'inter-community singing' is joined by other colonies anywhere up to a kilometre or more away—as far away as they and I can hear depending on the stillness of the night. These *sounds of majesty* are stunning in their beauty. If there is such a thing as angels singing (and I believe there is), the sound would have to be of this quality. They lift the soul into another place, out of the sometimes—dreary world of the daytime struggle and, for all practical purposes, into heaven—that state where time and space and substance are arrested, and we are just pure being.

Certainly singing is a divine happening. Whether it's a person or magpies, there is something beyond our ability to grasp or explain in the wonder of singing; of music. The earth sings. The wind softly soughing through sheoak leaves, cicadas after a hot day, kangaroo feet padding solidly but softly on hardened earth, rain dripping, trickling, running, torrenting, waves crashing or 'psshh-ing' gently on the white sandy beaches, a cooking fire crackling comfortingly, or a wildfire roaring and exploding out of control. Dogs barking, babies gurgling, children laughing, women and men exchanging as they go about their daily business.

Sounds of your majesty come to me wherever I turn.
Even the babbling of babes and the laughter of children spell out your
name.

I'm a granddad now. What a joy that is. Last week I took my second grandson, Nathan, who is just 6 month old, for a walk around the streets in his stroller. Lately he's been in some pain with reflux, the medical people (and grandmothers) think. So he's not comfortable some of the time and the dear little man cries. When that gets wearing and there's nothing else that can be done to improve his comfort, someone takes him for a long walk around the streets. This time it was my pleasure. From the time we strapped him in and headed out the front door, he didn't complain once. I walked him for several kilometres over an hour and a half. He was wide awake the whole time. As is my practice when I walk the grandsons, when I'm not talking to them or commenting on what we're passing, I hum a simple, repetitive, chant melody that is bassy and soft. It helps me stay present and use the walk as a meditation rather than a chore, and it seems to be quieting to the boys. On this walk, little Nathan didn't vocalise a lot. He babbled a bit now and again. But several times as we walked he vocalised a strong 'ahhh' for an entire out-breath of between 6 and 10 seconds and more or less on one note. An early song and a delight to a granddad! I can't put into words how I experienced those 'baby-babblings' but they filled me with a joy that brought tears to my eyes and fire to my heart. In this little boy walking and singing with his granddad, I experienced a God-happening.

When I gaze into star-printed skies,
The work of your fingers enfolds me, in amazement I stand.
For what I am I, my master, that you should watch over
And care for me.

Lying on my back on the grass looking up into the night sky, I am amazed again and again. But, more amazing to the observer is that God *'would watch over and care'* for him or her. Why would the Great Power of the universe be concerned for a few atoms of matter that is me? When I first think about that, it's beyond my understanding. But then I think about our own children, Emma and Ben and, even I, an ordinary, flawed human father would readily give all I could for them to be cared for. Anything less just isn't a consideration. I am their father and something in me goes out to them. I think it's the same with God. Something in

God automatically goes out to the creatures he created and loves. There is no other option. In fact, rather than 'going out to them', it's probably more accurate to say that because they came from him and through him and are sustained in union with him, they are inseparable. So they and God are not two, but One. There is no space between them. I feel that with our kids. They are of my substance and essence (and their mother's, of course)! Why wouldn't we *'watch over and care for '* them? And God, being so much greater than us, why wouldn't God *watch over and care for* you and me?

Why do we readily provide care and love for our children, but so many of us refuse to accept that there is one above us who provides care and love for us? Where did we get our ability and desire to care and love anyway? It's our strongest motivation and we didn't put it there. Accepting that there is One greater than us is often a difficult journey to make. The reasons for the difficulty would take many books, and writers far more skilled than I am. But I need to say a few words about it here. It's something to do with ego and fear. The great religious wisdom traditions agree on the central belief that there are two people in each of us; a lower self and a Higher Self. These are called various names and the names don't matter.As I mentioned in the introduction, I'll call the lower self 'ego', and the Higher Self 'True Self'. The ego is the temporal 'me' part and recipient of life; the True Self is the eternal "I AM' part—the God part—and is in union with the provider of life.

Although the ego is the essential agent for engaging with the external aspects of life in the physical world, if it is allowed free reign, it is also subject to deception and darkness. The True Self lives in truth and light. The ego likes and needs to attach to things and to hide things, pretend, justify, blame, rationalize, talk itself up, and many other devious games—mostly out of conscious awareness. In this excruciatingly bound-up way of living, the ego thinks it is free and powerful and cool!

The True Self is the opposite: it attaches to nothing, brings everything into the open, has no secrets, is only real, doesn't even know how to blame, criticize, rationalize, brag, etc; all it knows is how to 'be' True. The unconscious is brought into consciousness, light is shone on darkness, love dissolves fear. The True Self doesn't even think 'cool/un-cool'. It has no such concept. And, paradoxically, the True Self is *actually* 'cool'!, ie, exciting, strong, gentle, peaceful, joyful, patient, kind, self-controlled, faithful. You may care to read about these characteristics in a letter Paul wrote to the Christians in the city of Corinth (Bible:1 Corinthians 12). A person who is showing even the beginnings of these characteristics is experienced as awesome and wonderful. How much more wonderful is the One in whom these are perfected?

Wonder, how full of wonder
Splendour, how full of splendour you are

The way we perpetuate political management—I can't call it leadership—in our western nations these days is a pale, almost unrecognizable version of crowning a new king. Our leaders seem to have abandoned almost every decent quality in favour of cleverness, manipulation, deception, personal wealth and power (or the illusion of it), and every other so-called 'sophisticated' high-tech trick in order to rule the nation. So, to illustrate the point I'd like to make, we need to take an example from story-books and history.

Imagine a coronation ceremony. A prince is being crowned king. All the wealth of the kingdom, all the honour, all the glory, all the power now belongs to him. He is the authority in the land and everyone acknowledges him as the rightful ruler. He is the flesh and blood of his father; he is the rightful child and heir of the king. He is like his father. Trained in the skills of warfare, educated and groomed in matters of politics, philosophy, religion, leadership, courage, honour and serving the people in his care, he has become like his father. His father proudly calls him 'my son; my child'.

Although God's Kingdom is nothing like the one described above, the same sense of Kingdom glory being made available to those who belong to the Kingdom is parallel. Each one of us in this human race is like that prince or princess being crowned king or queen. Few people, if any, have ever told us that and demonstrated it in ways that enable us to believe it as truth. Most of us received mixed messages from our parents and carers. We were the apple of their eye one minute, and a 'wicked child' the next. Our inner conflicts began early and those two people I mentioned began taking up residence in opposition to each other from the beginning. There's much conjecture about whether we were born evil and can be transformed and made good again, or whether we are born good, get damaged and become evil, and can be made good again. The arguments are irrelevant. They will only serve to distract us from the real task. What is crucial, is that we come to realize and appropriate for ourselves the truth that God, in revelations like the Psalms, has expressed about our state and relationship with God:

You have crowned me with glory and made me so like you
That you even call me your child
Into my care you gave all the works of your hands,
You gave it to me

The suffering in our world will not end until we realize this truth about who we all are and start living accordingly from our Love centre instead of our fear periphery.

. . . .

Chapter Ten

Turn Around

The world will say, if something feels good, do it
The world will say you call the shots, you life's your own
But the day is coming when you have to stand up for what you are
You'll look to world to help you and you'll find you're on your own.

Turn around, you still have time
Don't believe you can do what you like
Don't believe it'll be alright, you're so wrong
Open you eyes, take hold of the life that is yours and mine
Turn around, turn around, you still have time

The world will say this life's all there is, so grab what you can
The world will say there's no right or wrong, your choice is free.
But the moment is near when you pass through the time that you
thought was the end
And where you are you'll find you're not where you want to be

Copyright: John White, 1986

Not too long ago it was common to hear—particularly young—people say, *'if it feels good, do it'*! Though this phrase is not so overtly used today the sentiment behind it, although expressed with far more subtlety is, perhaps, even stronger. In our world there are so-called developed nations, developing nations, and third world nations. The least fortunate are, of course, the people of the third world nations. Generally these nations have many people and few resources. In many cases the resources they had have been plundered by the so-called developed nations of the west. I say so-called because, in reality, the western nations have developed only their ability to manipulate whatever is necessary in order to feed their greed. There is little 'developed' in a people who think the purpose of humanity is to consume. These people are physically much more comfortable than their brothers and sisters in the poor nations. But they are no less poor and may be even poorer in the ways it matters most, ie, the ways of moral and ethical living; of spirit that produces justice, mercy and compassion.

All life is sacred. All human beings are of equal worth. To not know and live that it is to be truly poor; unaware and lost in the imaginings of the ego. Sages say the unaware life is not worth living.

In the song, *'Turn Around'*, 'the world' is mentioned. This is taken to be the political, economic, and social systems devised by mankind in the so-called developed and developing societies. Because of the faulty premise that economic structures and processes now started must not be interfered with, the 'markets' are, effectively, revered as God, and the result is that the vast majority of human beings on the planet are now slaves to the very systems we created to serve humanity. One aspect of this ridiculous and naïve belief about markets is that continued growth is possible in a finite eco-system. Any reasonably alert 5 year old will tell you that if you have 5 jelly beans, you can't give 10 children one each. So, because of these dramatically flawed beliefs underlying the foundations of our western-style societies, the physical, psychological and emotional life of every human being is compromised. We have allowed ourselves to be seduced into accepting the lie about growth and the resultant human good. History is clear that beyond a small increase in overall standard of living for the least fortunate, further economic growth does not flow down or even trickle down. Rather, it simply accumulates in the hands of a diminishing few. Because of the beliefs of those in power, the physical destiny of humanity at large is anything but attractive.

It is interesting to note that spirituality is generally stronger amongst the materially poor. Although there's nothing particularly desirable or noble about being poor, for many it has the benefit of refocussing themselves on traditional aspects of life other than material acquisition; culture, family, natural environment, matters of religion and spirit have been life for thousands of years. Only in the last few hundred years have we sped away from ancient values.

Of course, when deprivation is extreme, people find it almost impossible to focus on anything other than mere survival. Such poverty in this world is an obscenity and a great shame of humanity.

However, there are and have always been those individuals who are informed from within that life is not only about body and mind but, finally, about spirit. And they are found in isolation in every culture and nation and time. Of course there are millions attending churches. mosques, synagogues, temples and meetings of all kinds who are seeking the spirit life. Unfortunately, the human-made systems associated with these religious sects and denominations can restrict the free movement of the Spirit. We seem to be unable to break free from rituals, regulations, structures and procedures which are far more to do with our egos than with the freedom of the life-giving Spirit. I do not use the term 'ego' in a derogatory sense. Ego is that part of the human psyche that necessarily interacts with the day to day world and keeps us safe—especially when we are growing from childhood to adulthood. The tragedy is that most adults don't become aware that this ego is not who they really are at essence, so they never find and grow into their True Selves. Not only are they not safe in the ego, they are, in fact, imprisoned securely by it.

Many who think they have found the way, have only found 'a way to the Way'. Most are not aware of this reality. Many spend well-intentioned but less than fully effective lives in religious activity of one kind or another, wearing out the body and mind and perhaps not nourishing the spirit as much as would be beneficial. We see this when we consider that justice, mercy and compassion are central to producing life and peace for all, yet many of these different groups engage in excluding and even violent action against others and the created order in the name of God, Jesus, Allah, or some other personally projected deity.

Can we move from '*a* way' to actually engage with "*the* Way"? Is there such a thing as '*the* Way'? There are some who say that most of us don't want to become aware and wake up and see who we really are and what life is all about. We're comfortable asleep. I believe that's true. Anthony de Mello says *'we're born in our sleep, we marry in our sleep, we have children in our sleep and we die in our sleep".* (Awareness) If people were awake in great numbers, the world would not be experiencing the awful human obscenities of war, famine, wholesale destruction of environments, poverty and abuses of every kind. There are many in churches who say 'you must be born again'. I agree. But what does it mean? Does it mean to say some magic words and everything is new? I don't think so. I think it means 'wake up and see correctly, and live according to that new sight'. And the only way to wake up is to willingly draw on, and allow ourselves to be drawn by and into, the mysterious power of Love that we may choose to call God, and which dwells in the innermost parts of each of us.

And when we wake up and can see for the first time, we *'turn around'*. And it doesn't just happen once. It is a process as continuous as the tide of our breath from the first to the last. We are encouraged to *'be filled with the Holy Spirit'(Bible: Ephesians. 5:18)* day after day. Gurus, prophets, mystics, wisdom seekers throughout the history of humanity agree on the basics. If we don't engage the physical world with reference to a greater, mysterious, spirit reality, this world is *maya;* illusion. It may come as a shock to think that what we accept as being real, insofar as it is considered without reference to anything other than itself, it is illusory. But a quick reflection on the fragility and finiteness of this physical existence as human beings, and on the never ending, indomitable power of Love and faith that transcend intellectual and physical proof, will tell you that the physical world is only part of Reality. So to place our trust and hope and energies solely into this physical existence to the exclusion of anything more profound is, simply, folly and death when what we wanted and thought we were getting was life. This is another tragedy, but one that can be reversed if we choose to wake up and *'turn around.'*

This song was written at a time when our group of friends was being taught by John Abraham, a wonderful, wise man who had chosen the Christ-path through life. Love and light and wisdom were being taught and practised. This was not just mental assent to rules and regulations; this was an experienced surrender to a deeper inner presence that provided the power to give life to the words and actions we were hearing from and seeing in John. This was an exciting time and one of the times I turned around again. At that time my theology was rudimentary and largely flavoured by the traditional teaching of the Anglican Church. In the song you may see what appears to be a reference to an unpleasant place that comes after death. I believe that heaven and hell are in this life and are 'eternal' in the sense of being 'timeless'. Scripture tells us that *"the kingdom of God is within you'* (*Bible:* Luke 17:21) here and now. The moment I wake up and turn around, I can see and experience it. I am there now, and there is here, right where I am, in this very breath that I am breathing as long as I am aware of that great Reality. The more useful interpretation of this line is that because of our choices we often end up in situations in life in which we don't want to be.

It may be that many in the Christian faith—and any other faith for that matter—don't reflect upon or contemplate our beliefs to any great extent. I think we start out genuinely seeking, and when we encounter what we experience to be God, we embrace that new reality with great and real joy. That seems to be the time when the main direction we receive and, thus, the one we take leads us to study to learn more but, primarily, with the mind. Yet the mind is only one facet of us that needs to be turned around. The will, the soul, the body, the heart, the spirit—all of me—needs to be turned around and made new. In some wisdom traditions it is said that 'beyond the senses is the mind, beyond the mind is reason, and beyond reason is Truth'. Many wise women and men through history agree with this movement of knowing and surrendering as we journey towards life and truth.

Let's look at the lyrics and talk a bit more about this turning around.

As adults we learn that things that feel good, taste good, look good, smell good, etc, are not necessarily good or right for us. *"If it feels good, do it'* is the childish ego speaking, and more dangerous and destructive than we will ever know in this life. In the restorative justice prison work with which I am involved at the moment, one of the key messages in the programme is that every action has implications far beyond our ability to see. Every criminal action has numberless victims. The programme is called The Sycamore Tree Project, and is based on the biblical story of the encounter between Jesus and a hated, Roman-tax collector whose name was Zacchaeus. In the encounter, the non-judgemental but challenging approach of Jesus enabled Zacchaeus to wake up, see what he had become, and turn his life around. The programme's success is based on the non-judgemental, supportive challenge in the stories of the team members who have suffered as victims of crime. These experiences are shared with a volunteer group of offenders who are still in prison (not the ones who offended against the team members).

This small, temporary community built on non-judgement, supportive challenge, personal responsibility, honesty, honour for all humans as equals, confidentiality, etc, produces an environment in which all can be themselves with safety. Psychological games are progressively dropped and participants become real. As they share their stories of pain and hurt, a bond of genuine compassion and human connection develops in which past hurts related to criminal activity can be allowed to begin dissolving and, in their place, a new healing and peace enabled to grow.

In this community of love and truth, each person develops a new awareness that we are all one, and when we commit an offence there are many victims including the one offending. There are some delightful moments. One young man in a group of predominantly violent offenders thought of himself as 'not really into crime'. He was a drug dealer and, in his mind, there were 'no victims'! One of our team members, with tears of agony and rage, told the story of her son who had become hooked on 'ice' and had taken his own life. At the end of that session, this young drug offender announced to the group, 'I have learned that drug dealers are criminals and I have victims'! There was great applause and serious mirth all round. He had woken up to one issue and had turned around his thinking, at least, about this one. *'You call the shots, your life's your own'*. Someone said 'there are four things you need to know before you can really begin to live: 1. life is hard. 2. you're going to die. 3. You have no control over that or almost anything else. 4. Your life's not even about you. My life is not my own. Everything I think, say and do has an impact on every other creature in this closed system called planet earth of which I am a part. Our task in life is to wake up and become aware of the complexity of the interconnectedness of all life in order that we may live in ways that are life-giving and life-preserving to the whole planetary community.

'But the day is coming when you have to stand up for what you are'. You may take this as a reference to the biblical 'judgement day' when all will be called to account for their personal lives. There may be a judgement day. I don't know. But I think it is more likely to be true that every day—every moment, in fact—is judgement day, and every moment we are to be aware that we are accountable for that moment and it's implications for others and for life generally. As we practise awareness of everything within and around us, we become progressively more aware of the implications of every action of every being, and that awareness has a profound guiding towards right action in everything we think, say and do. As this may be my only day remaining, there is nothing better for me to do that live it with integrity, with honour and with love for all creation. If I choose not to, but *'look to the world to help . . . '* or answer for me, I'll find I'm on my own. This is not to say that we are isolated beings and not part of the world and each other. As I have said elsewhere, we are inextricably linked to all life. Rather it is referring to the fact that another cannot help me in the sense of releasing me from the responsibility for my actions. The world can't absolve me. The old saying 'you can run but you can't hide' is true. I can't blame, justify, or rationalise my deeds away from me. I can't hide behind anything or anyone else in this world. There is no dodging personal responsibility for my life and all my choices. Three good words to learn and use always

are 'I am responsible'. I read on a poster in a school today, 'make an effort . . . not an excuse'.

Turn around, you still have time. If you reflect for a moment you may find that what you're doing is causing pain or damage to another person, another creature, yourself, or some other part of the eco-systems of the world. If you are, there's something you can do at any time. It is never too late. To knowingly continue causing destruction of any degree, is to destroy yourself in the process and, thus, not be the wonderful, whole, unique creature that you are designed to be. We delude ourselves if we think we can '*do what we like . . . it'll be alright . . . '* we simply can't. Wisdom is like gravity; it cannot be changed, it can only be demonstrated. You may not believe in it, but jump out of a tall tree and you'll discover the reality of gravity. The same with wisdom; attempt to defy it, and you will only cause destruction to all involved in your defiant actions.

What can we do?

Open your eyes, take hold of the life that is yours and mine'.

There is an inner life that few, if any, ever fully discover. This inner life causes people to love and give and heal and work selflessly for justice with mercy and compassion equally for all. These souls have woken up and can see with eyes of the heart; they see correctly. They are not concerned for the trappings (literally) of this consuming society, because they see the meaninglessness of it all. Their concern is for life in all its fullness; life for everyone; a decent standard of living, clean water, security for all people and for their children, peace and joy and love instead of violence and misery and fear. At any moment anyone can *take hold of this* (spirit) *life that is yours and mine.* It is the wonderful birthright of every human being. We refuse it for ourselves to our peril and the peril of the human race. I recently heard the wonderful, wise and compassionate Mohammad Younis—a Nobel Peace Prize winner—say, *'making money is very exciting; changing the world is much more exciting'!*

The reason human society and other ecosystems we inhabit are disintegrating quite rapidly, is that we have been conned into listening to the ego (the voice of the superficial world) rather than to the True Self of our inner being. This ego convinces us that *'this life's all there is, so grab what you can'. 'There's no right or wrong, your choice is free'.* Grabbing what we can has taken wholesome food and clean water from the mouths of countless millions of our brothers and sisters in this one family to which we all belong. Sure, our choice is free! But it is intended that we exercise it with wisdom and compassion, with awareness of the impact we have at every action. This free choice some of us in the privileged parts of the world have been exercising has denuded and salinised the landscape so much of it won't produce anything. This free choice has added to the delicately balanced eco-systems of this planet billions of tonnes of waste materials that the earth doesn't know what to do with. There is no waste in nature! Everything is recycled. The extent to which we will not recycle and reduce our waste to zero, is the extent to which we are surely driving this planet towards the point at which it may eject us and countless millions of other species. Scientists, and the silent witness of the earth itself, tell us there have been five or six previous extinction events in the history of the earth. They also tell us that we are in the next extinction event right now, and the current one will be the first one caused by the human species. So we need to be careful how much we grab and how we exercise our wonderful free choice, or *'where you are you'll find you're not where you want to be'.*

Our task is to assess where right-acting, mature human beings with integrity, honour and love should be at any given moment, and then choose to be there now and always. In regard to being *'where we want to be'* both in the basic habitability of the planet and in the spiritual unity for which we are designed, our task is similar; a moment by moment awareness of our focus and actions, and the effects they have on all other creatures and on ourselves. But it is important to remember that we can't achieve any of the above with only our egos, minds and bodies. It is only the deep, mysterious, inner Spirit that is able to effect anything of significance. It is only *'the spirit that gives life'* (2 Corinthians 3:6) And it is only be accepting this reality and surrendering all of ourselves to it that frees it to produce life in us and all others around us.

So, if you haven't already, turn around!

Chapter Eleven

The Sky's No Limit.

In recent times, the dangers of allowing the market to have its head have become even more painfully evident. Some months ago in Australia we had runaway development in the resources sector fuelling China's insatiable appetite for raw materials and energy. Resource companies needed to attract more labour. Huge salaries were being paid to the few who worked in that field. Rents and house prices went skyward as highly paid workers were prepared to pay anything to secure accommodation. Landlords, developers and real estate agents succumbed to greed, happy to cash in on the unprecedented demand. Non-resource sector workers could no longer afford to buy or even rent a home.

Our recently-married son has decided not to even consider entering the rat race of this stupidity. Instead of spending the rest of his life with his 'masculinity' in a bank vault until he pays off a $500,000 loan three or four times over, he has decided to build a yacht to become his mobile family home. Using recycled materials as much as possible, and the good hand skills he has that any man or woman can learn and develop, he and Kylie will have a modest living space, debt-free within the two or three years it will take to construct it.

Not everyone wants to live on a yacht and sail the world. But it's a valid and interesting option. They want to be free of the life-limiting constraints prescribed by our society and controlled by the markets that oppose uniqueness, suffocate creativity and crush human potential. They want to see the wonders of creation in a way that's affordable in financial and ecological terms, and combines adventure, accommodation, and development of their spiritual, mental, emotional and physical capacities.

The paragraphs above are preamble to the following statements which, themselves, are preamble to the matters being considered in this chapter.

At the beginning of a simple, extraordinary book called *'Buehler's Backyard Boatbuilding'*—the initial research for our son's build—these extraordinary, ordinary words are written:

'To all people who aren't afraid to do or think things for themselves, and thereby keep this world from becoming too boring'. (Buehler. Ragged Mountain, 1991)

'The years thunder by. The dreams of youth grow dim where they lie caked in dust on the shelves of Patience. Before we know it, the tomb is sealed'. (Sterling Hayden in Buehler))

These words are striking. They are also tragic indicators of the world and life we create for ourselves; a world grotesquely distorted by fear-filled lives eked out at or below the lowest common denominator. Very few have found within themselves the truth about their humanity; that profound, unique, divine creative spirit that calls them to live fully and freely and never be restricted by the mass hysteria that has claimed most others and limited them to sameness with everyone else. This is perhaps the greatest human tragedy from which all other tragedies spring. It is probably alsot true to call it 'sin'; ie, living less than the divinely instilled possibility.(Buehler)

I quote these short statements in the hope that they will inspire us all to reconsider how we're living and make necessary adjustments while there is time and life to do so. Someone else said 'I'd rather die on my feet than live on my knees'. Because of resigned adherence to the demands of the market systems, many of us live on our knees for our entire lives; most of us limit ourselves to scratching around in the dirt.

At the beginning of this book I quoted a traditional story about the eagle that was raised with chickens, and lived and died as a chicken never realizing who it was nor achieving its potential to soar majestically through life.

This book and CD is part of my contribution to there being more eagles and less chickens.

You've probably heard stories of people being given the 'opportunity of a lifetime' to do this or that. Often the one promoting the opportunity to them says, 'the sky's the limit'! According to the sentiment expressed in the above story, the limit is what our minds decide is the limit. So I'd like to suggest to you that even the sky is no limit unless you think it is. Whilst most people accept that high flying supersonic aircraft are the limit for aviation, Sir Richard Branson is now providing opportunities for people to fly in space. The sky's no limit unless you decide it is. Of course there are universal laws that set certain physical limits. But we generally don't get anywhere near those limits; we apply far more restriction to our physical activity than universal laws ever apply to us.

What I hope we can consider in this discussion, is that physical laws are of a lower order than spiritual laws. When we allow ourselves to be fully embraced by or immersed in what we have, throughout this book, called God, there are limits only to our physical nature, and that is not the real you or me. Those who have developed their intellectual abilities may not agree. The human ego is formidable. This is no criticism; it is just fact. The satisfaction and defence of the human ego is a powerful force that is the underbelly of the Western, economic-rationalistic nations wherever they are on the planet. People who value the intellect above all else are simply those who have been seduced by the populist view that the mind is the greatest faculty of humankind. All great wisdom traditions agree that using our physical and intellectual faculties only, it is not possible to reach Truth; the mystery, the wonder of life is far beyond our human understanding. If you are one of those described above, I affirm you for your diligence and effort in developing your powers of reason as much as you are able. I also invite you to surrender them to the greater power of Spirit in order to do something of immeasurably greater value to yourself and to humankind. Be reminded that the great wisdom traditions agree that *'higher than the mind is reason, higher than reason is Truth'. 'My thoughts are higher than your thoughts and my ways than your ways, says the Lord' (Isaiah 55:9)*

In 25 years of practising psychotherapy, I've been fortunate to have met thousands of wonderful, creative, alive people who, because of the people they lived with as children, or because of the impact upon them of the behaviour of others or of life's events, had that wonder, creativity and life smothered and denied to the extent that it no longer appeared. It was certainly present in-utero and, for most, at birth because it is our nature—our essence as beings. My belief and experience is that it is alive and potential as long as our spirit gives us breath. It may be of interest to consider that 'breath' translates as 'Spirit'. Our challenge is to help everyone including ourselves to clear the debris of the brokenness, unlearn the lies that we learned, and allow the truth of our unique beauty and wonder to be once more revealed. Our challenge is to make real—to experience—the limitlessness that is our Essence. If, as major wisdom traditions suggest, it is true that we are part of the cosmic Oneness of all things seen and unseen, we are beyond time and space. And matter. Science tells us that every atom of our being has been through at least three supernovas. We are, truly, 'stardust'; timeless, spaceless, matter-less at essence. We simply 'are'. That means there are no limits. Not even the sky!

If that's the case, why is it not the experience of the average person? Why don't we feel limitless and achieve limitlessly? Why do we get sick and depressed and angry and anxious and all the other feelings it's possible for the human being to experience? Could it be that, from even before birth, we began experiencing those limits mediated through the sounds and movements and energies in and around us? Could it be that, even before birth, our limitless spirit was burdened and blocked by events outside our physical selves without either our consent or ability to do anything about it? I believe that's what happened and continues to happen generation after generation. It is written in Scriptures *'the sins of the fathers (*and mothers) *will be visited on the children to the third and fourth generations'.* (Ex.20:5)

Our sisters and brothers in the east talk about 'karma'—effect; there is a direct link in the Universal Laws of action and effect. We cannot do anything without our actions having an effect. The nature of the effect is really up to us. If we are aware of the implications of our actions, we can change our future. Even if we can't change certain events, we can change our response to them. That is effect.

Our 'karma' starts early in our lives—even before birth.

Words you heard, faces you saw
Stole the power that would have made you more
Than anyone thought possible
They were paralysed by fear
Afraid to be different, to be free

Your spirit broken when you were young
A song in you waits to be sung
A mighty symphony, meant to shake the earth
Splendour dies at birth

But the sky's no limit, believe the sky's no limit
Know the sky's no limit for you, no limit for you
No limit for you

The sky's no limit when you're free
Free to become what you can be
Break now the chains that shackle your mind
The sky's no limit for you

On wings you rise free and strong
Beyond the sky is where you belong
Reach out it may be yours, lose not a moment more
There is no limit for you

Copyright: White/Stedman 1989

We don't have the capacity here to consider our pre-birth experiences and their effect on us as maturing beings. But we can consider the experiences since birth from as early as we can remember. In my psychotherapy experience, I have found these words to be accurate:

Words you heard, faces you saw
Stole the power that would have made you more
Than anyone thought possible . . .

Imagine yourself, if you will, as a small, totally dependent baby looking up at a loving, smiling face speaking tender words of love and care and value, gentle and strong arms holding you securely yet freely, clothing softly and comfortably keeping the temperature at the optimum level for you. You experience safety, warmth, supply of your needs; all is well with you. You feel you are one with all that's around you. You are at rest, at peace. I really hope that was your experience. For most of us it probably wasn't.

* Now imagine yourself as a small, totally dependent baby lying somewhere uncomfortable, knowing something is terribly wrong because you feel pain of aloneness, coldness, wetness, hunger, what you want and need is not being provided. You scream in distress. But, instead of being made comfortable, you feel rough violent hands throwing you around, striking you, bending and breaking you, and loud, harsh, terrifying voices saying words you don't understand but inherently know are desperately dangerous to you. You feel terror. And you are powerless to do anything about it. That makes it even more terrifying. Perhaps you don't have to imagine that experience. Perhaps something of that was your experience. Because I am your brother, I am grieved by that terror inflicted on you without you understanding it, deserving it, or being able to accommodate it in your beautiful, tiny, fragile person. I weep at the shame of those who inflicted it.

These are the 'words you heard, faces you saw that stole the power that would have made you more than anyone thought possible'. These are the words and faces of inhumanity that placed the earliest limits on your wonder-full self. Until you heard and saw these terrible things, there was just glorious, limitless humanity in baby form. The next words, although of little comfort to you perhaps even now, explain in some way the reason behind the disgraceful treatment you experienced from those who were meant to care for, love and nurture you.

They were paralysed by fear, afraid to be different, to be free.

To be able to see this truth may be some way off for the person who has shut away their pain in an attempt to get on with life. When this happens—and often it seems to be the only available solution to the young one who is suffering—healing can only begin when these feelings of violation are allowed to resurface and be experienced.

You just can't see clearly with pain you've pushed down inside. It is the filter through which all of your life is viewed and experienced. You certainly can't see your abuser with compassion until you have been allowed to feel your pain (including and especially being allowed by yourself) and have that pain validated by a safe, loving human being. There is no point in trying to 'put it behind you' and 'get on with your life' until this limiting pain has been allowed to be named, expressed in some appropriate way and, over time, integrated to the point where its memory no longer causes you unmanageable distress.

After a time, when we are feeling a bit more human, stronger, able to cope with whatever comes along, there is another major task to achieve before we can say we are healed and free of what was done to us. And it's probably more appropriate to say reasonably healed and healing, because complete healing doesn't come in this lifetime on earth. That task is to be able to see with eyes and hearts of compassion, those who abused us and caused us suffering. As hard as it may be to stomach this, there are powerful reasons for our abusers behaving in the way they did towards us. We have to be able to see the damage done to them as youngsters, that made it possible for them to do what they did to us. This may seem a big ask. But, if we want to be healed and free to live a fully human life, it's not an option; sooner or later we have to do it or we remain stuck in the mess caused by those others. That means they continue to run our lives.

If you are experiencing a strong negative reaction to what you just read—if you are resisting what I have suggested—you almost certainly need to spend some more time talking and working through the pain of your past with someone skilled, before you are able to read and benefit from what comes next. By all means, read on, but be aware of what's happening inside you as you do. If what you read isn't readily acceptable, realize the feeling is arising within you; you need to own it; it's not about the material you're reading. It's about something in you that needs some attention.

Here we need to pray for, to seek power beyond ourselves in order to even consider this past suffering as somehow having an understandable beginning. And this is usually not something that is easily or quickly done, or done alone.

Put simply, although there are no excuses for what evil was done to us as children, there are explanations. If we can manage to put our pain aside just for a moment—not deny or dismiss it, but, rather, see past it rather than through it—and try to put ourselves in the place of our abusers when they were children, we may just get an insight that will help us be released from our own suffering. We may even engage our compassion for the past suffering of those who hurt us. When that happens, we are on the way to healing and wholeness and life as it was meant to be.

Consider, if you will, the paragraph above marked with an asterisk (*) as describing the childhood experience of those who were responsible for giving you care. If they were treated in this way, they, too, suffered as you did. They, too, had no ability to change what was happening to them. They, too, learned nothing but pain and harshness and violence and worthlessness, and had nothing life-giving to give to you; nothing of tenderness, gentleness, personal value with which to provide the same for you. In short, they didn't know how to love you. They were doing the best they could and it was pretty inadequate. But, if it was the best they could do, how can we continue to hate and despise them for what they inflicted on us; what they, at some level, couldn't avoid doing? They didn't know they were *paralysed by fear*, they didn't know there *was* anything different from what they knew, and they didn't know anything about being free. They thought—and maybe still think—they are free, as so many people of our world do. But their lives demonstrate that they are the most pitiful prisoners of all; imprisoned in the fear of their egos, the brokenness of their psyches, and ignorance of what it means to be human.

And so, *your spirit broken when you were young* is a great and terrible fact under the limiting suffering of billions of damaged human beings, the damage created by billions of well-meaning but similarly damaged people. I encourage you to strive with all you are, to move away from and beyond the fact of damage that was done to you, because, in the vast majority of situations, it was done by unaware adults who themselves were so damaged they really had no option. This does not minimise your real suffering or their real guilt. They were responsible for their actions at all times, and they were given inadequate tools to be able to do anything different from what they did. This difficult fact leaves us all in the same boat. We are all both producers of damage to others, and sufferers of damage at the hands of others. It's just a matter of degree. When we begin to see that, great release and freedom is experienced within us.

This new way of seeing can take a great deal of our lifetime. It is important not to attempt to push it at a pace unnatural to our individual, personal process. What is absolutely essential to do, is to notice what's happening, name it, own it as your own personal reaction at this present moment of your life, and breathe this breath; be present to this breath. The last one is gone forever, the next one can't come yet, this breath is the only breath I can actually take; the only one I can be aware of and present to. And this breath is charged with the life-giving, spirit-energy of God who, as our ancient Indian sisters and brothers have said is 'the breath within the breath'. Practise being aware in this way and, in time, a new way of being and seeing will arise from within the depths of your soul. A new quality of life and peace and joy will start to bubble. And with it you will notice that you are experiencing greater well-being. As many of the wise women and men through history have said, you'll be 'waking up'. You could call this being 'born again' by an inner power that you might choose to call the Spirit of God or some other word attempting to express the inexpressible. The name is unimportant. What is essential is that this inner life-stream is acknowledged as being THE truth about existence. The western Christian tradition links this truth to the arrival in time and space of the person of Jesus Christ who announced this new way of being. He called it the 'Kingdom of God' as opposed to the kingdom of the world and of mankind, and he said *'it is within you'*. (Luke 17:21). It was and is a Spirit reality. In every religious tradition it is this same Spirit reality, although not all acknowledge it as such. It is *the* life-giving power. There is no other way to be fully alive than to surrender to and flow with this life in all its fullness. To attempt to manufacture our own version of life is to remain sick, suffering, broken.

That *'song in you waits to be sung'*. The evidence provided by thousands of years of observing humankind indicates that there is great diversity in our race. It seems that, like snow flakes, no human being is exactly like any other human being. We are unique. Like threads in a tapestry, we each have a specific place and equal worth in the whole fabric. Each of us has a specific place in life; a purpose to fulfil that will fulfil us. A song to sing, if you like. The greatest challenge seems to be to not forget your lyrics and melody in the push of the world to make you fit in with the rest; to make you not stand out and be seen and heard in your unique difference and richness. The ones who run the world are afraid of difference because difference can't be predicted or controlled. The ones who run the systems of the world can't risk wild cards spoiling their plans to be wealthy and powerful and in control. They need their wealth and power to provide them the illusion of being successful, significant and secure human beings. They need their material endeavours to provide a distraction from the deep, relentless, vehemently resisted inner unrest that knows they are none of these things.

If you sang your song and everyone else sang their songs, what a cacophony there would be! How could the noise be directed? How could it be moved and channelled? And so you see, the world systems of control and power cannot dare allow you to sing your song. These systems will certainly not encourage you to sing your song. And the world is dying of mediocrity, apathy and boredom because of it. People are dying of distress, depression and despair because of it. People are expressing their frustration of uniqueness and personal worth being denied in ways that are socially and individually destructive. The world's problems exist because people are not being celebrated for singing their God-given songs. The world has become largely beige and boring and going nowhere good. You must find your song and sing it boldly. You will not be well until you do. You'll not be free and alive.

It's true that when we start touching our inner Self, a personal, unique reality begins to be experienced. It is true that in each person born there is a *mighty symphony, meant to shake the earth.* A degree of literary license has been taken here. A symphony may not *shake* the earth, but it will certainly have an impact upon it! And we know that a symphony does not come from an individual, but is a composition of many individual sounds working in cooperation and under the artistic direction of a musically gifted leader who draws out each part and weaves them into a magnificent, single whole sound. But although each of us can only play a part in such an external symphony there is, also, a symphony to be produced within each individual; a work comprising the harmonious interplay of the myriad aspects of each human being. If to sing your song means to be and express who *you* really are, then to deny any part of that expression is to saboutage the production and prevent it from becoming the great work it was dreamed to be.

And when this great inner symphony, and part of even greater outer symphonies is denied, *splendour dies;* the glory that is full, free humanity dies or, at least, suffers dramatically. Such tragedy is played out every time a baby is born and not nurtured, treasured and loved. Such tragedy is played out every time a child or adult is abused or neglected in some way. Our world is filled with such tragedy because we are not sufficiently encouraged to know who we really are as individuals and unique, essential parts of the greater oneness of humanity and creation. We are not encouraged to know we are glorious, Eternal Spirit Being in physical form for this part of our journey. We are not encouraged to know we are worthy, loved and equal, and can rest content and secure in that sure truth. Our task is to relocate that truth within ourselves, and sing the *song in you that waits to be sung,* making a *mighty symphony that will shake the earth,* giving it life and great goodness enabling it to continue its being.

The sky's no limit when you're free
Free to become what you can be
Break now the chains that shackle your mind
The sky's no limit for you

When we are freed from the constraints, lies, and manipulations of the world systems we have created, or allowed to be created through ignorance, powerlessness or apathy, when we see and know that Reality is eternal spirit in and through our material selves, we are freed from physical constraints. Even the sky is composed of atoms of physical matter, and the physical cannot impose itself upon the spirit. It is the spirit/matter combination or continuum that is fullness of life

It says in biblical Scripture, '*if the Son shall make you free, you shall be free indeed'(John 8:36)*. The historic Christ was alluding to this fact of his and, thus, our transcendent, spirit nature; to know this as he knew it was to be free indeed.

This chapter has been about seeing differently; waking up and becoming aware that we have placed or allowed others to place various *shackles* on us that have limited our lives and made us to some degree ineffectual. Sure there have been great achievements throughout history. And all of the truly great ones have been characterised by great love. Anything achieved without this great love is flawed at its core. *'Unless God (Spirit) builds, we labour in vain' (Psalm 127:1)* One of the most significant ways we have been shackled is in our thinking; in our minds. We have bought the lie that our intellectual abilities are the highest we have. I said elsewhere that many wisdom traditions agree that first come senses, then mind, then reason, then Truth which is only found by non-rational means and far beyond the reach of the intellect. Although the reason we have allowed this lie to shackle our minds is academic, nevertheless it is a fact. Our minds have been shackled and, with them, our souls and spirits that are the rest of the truth about us, and that live beyond time and space and anything physical or intellectual only.

On wings you rise free and strong
Beyond the sky is where you belong

Reach out it may be yours, lose not a moment more
There is no limit for you

There are some wonderful references in Scriptures to *rising up on wings, free and strong,* flying like eagles (Isaiah 40:31). These words inspire everyone who genuinely seeks wisdom in them; they carry the stamp of our nature, the purpose and being to which we are called and for which we are equipped. They carry our aspirations. How many of us ever look up at an eagle soaring above and not, at some stage in life, soar in our spirits and dreams with her? We paint pictures of flight, we build aircraft that fly ever higher and faster, we write songs about being lifted up by the Truth that is in us and *is* us (*love lift us up where we belong* . . .) And still we scratch around like the eagle in the chicken pen for our entire lives, never realizing and expressing more than a fraction of our magnificent potential as beings of transcendent love and spirit and abundant life.

And so we come to the end of this little journey together and the beginning of the rest of our life journeys. What we do with them is our choice. Whatever may have happened in the past must be resolved adequately and required to remain in the past. We are no longer there. We are here now. We must practise being here. With sufficient love it is possible for everyone to be enabled to once again be healed, safe, alive and here. Psychologists may argue that there are some who are so deeply wounded by past abuse that they will never recover. I have travelled with some of these brothers and sisters and it seems to be so—at least in the psychological / emotional sense. Maybe it was just that I didn't have enough love and wisdom and time to provide the kind of healing companionship they needed. Who can really say? I do know that I am always sad when I meet someone for whom there doesn't seem to be release. Maybe beyond this physical life is the resolution for these precious little ones. Maybe it is even now in ways we are unable to recognise. God knows.

But what we can all do as much as we are able, is to seek and hear the truth about us and refuse to continue listening to the lies that hold us back. We can question all assumptions that seem to leave us short of where we inwardly know we should be. We can seek out people who are seeking too, and travel together towards truth and freedom and life of peace and joy.

Reach out it may be yours, lose not a moment more
There is no limit for you

. . . the sky's no limit, believe the sky's no limit
Know the sky's no limit for you, no limit for you
No limit for you . . .

Conclusion

I hope that, having read this little book, and listened to the CD, *No Bars Hold,* you have at least caught a glimpse of, had a taste of, have heard or been touched by something of the great reality that we call God; the great reality in which we and all things seen and unseen exist. Indeed, it is not possible for us not to be in this reality, for it is the cradle in which the entire universe rests.

I hope you have experienced further release from your prisons, something of the indwelling Spirit of freedom and life, and you know where to search in order to satisfy the inner longing that we all experience simply because we are human.

I hope you experience and rest contentedly in your being made in the image of God, experience being loved as you are, and called ever deeper into the great mystery of life. I hope you know that any wanderings from the path of Life have only been temporary aberrations and, the instant you returned to the path, you are restored to life again, in union, at peace and safe once more.

I hope you have experienced and go on experiencing something of the wonder of life that is around and within us all at all times. And I hope you experience that, although we are limited by our material bodies, because we are also timeless spirits united with the infinite Spirit of God, in real terms there are no limits for the real you and me. We can rest peacefully in that inner knowing.

Vincent, a wise friend of mine, once said to me, 'don't follow the mind; it will take you down a dark alley and mug you'. Every anxiety, every suffering has a powerful connection to what we allow our minds to do. It seems to me that humans make two major errors with our thinking: we don't think at many times when that would be the best course of action; and we do think—or, rather, allow our minds to function unchecked—when it would be best to contain and gently discipline them. Wisdom literature says 'as we think, we are'. Shakespeare said 'there is nothing either good or bad but thinking makes it so'.

So, as we grow towards the fullness of our True Selves, we need to acknowledge that our minds alone will never get us there; our minds are finite. It is the soul or spirit—that deepest place in us—that is infinite. That place can only be entered beyond words and images in silence and stillness. The most commonly used pathway to that place is meditation. In its simplest definition, meditation is a method of passing beyond the constant distractions of the mind. There are no sinister associations with dangerous religions. Our simple, constant intent to become one with the God of all that is is enough to make the journey safe.

A Way to Meditate

Sit down. Sit still and upright. Sit in silence. Close your eyes lightly. Sit relaxed but alert. Silently, interiorly being to say a single word. We recommend the prayer phrase 'maranatha'. It is an Aramaic word meaning 'come Lord'. Used in this way it becomes a willing opening of your deepest Self to the Source of all things; of Love, Wisdom, Truth, Union, Being. Recite it as four syllables of equal length. You may find that two syllables as you draw breath and two syllables as you exhale will give you the simple rhythm that works best. Listen to it as you say it, gently but continuously.

You may prefer not to use a mantra but, rather, to just be aware of your breathing in and out. Do not think or imagine anything—spiritual or otherwise. If thoughts and images come, these are distractions at the time of meditation, so pay them no attention; just keep returning to simply saying the word or being aware of your breath. Meditate each morning and evening for between 20 and 30 minutes. (John Main, 'Word into Silence')

Healing begins with inner silence and stillness. You will probably find it helpful to at least begin with outer silence and stillness also. As we learn to sit, to be—silent and still—we detach from all the distractions of the mind and body, and are led into union with our True self, the Christ-nature within and, thus, to and the Ground of Universal Being whom we may reflect on as God. The deepest prayer, the deepest union, the richest life comes with inner silence and stillness.

Although silence and stillness may be easier for some than for others, everyone can learn this. Everyone needs to learn this. To be still and silent inwardly is to be removed from the attachments and busyness of our minds that keep us from truly 'being'. The important point to remember is that it's not a matter of being 'good at' meditation; it is a matter of simply, gently, continuously 'returning' our awareness to this present breath, this present spoken mantra, this present moment. It is important not to fight yourself. As soon as you become aware that your mind has wandered—and it will always to a greater or lesser extent—simply and lovingly (smilingly) return it to the focus of being right here and right now. Awareness of the activity of mind and consistent return from its distractions is all we need to do.

John White
Toodyay
August 2009

Further Reading

The Bullcreek / Leeming /Willetton parish was most 'un-Anglican'. At one stage the then-Archbishop was heard to remark that we were 'barely Anglican'. That didn't bother anyone very much. There was life in the Spirit there that we had never experienced before moving back to Perth from our teaching stint in the country and becoming part of that group. Part of what was different was that we were one of the first parishes at that time to use guitars and other modern instruments, and sing and write songs other than the traditional hymns that enabled us to worship God in an exuberant way. I suppose we could be called 'charismatic'. And because we got around to other Christian gatherings quite a bit, our music became known and we were often asked to provide music or lead worship at one place or another.

Winston and Ruth Bailey and I had led the music worship for a parish retreat at Dongara on the weekend of August 10th to 12th 1979. It was a fun-filled weekend of singing, dancing, praising, praying, eating, drinking, sharing and learning together with the people of the North Midlands and Morawa-Perenjori parishes.

At the conclusion of the weekend, we were each given a small gift as a token of their appreciation of what we had provided over the weekend. I was given a book by William Johnson called *'Silent Music'*. It was about the science of meditation. At that time, my Christian experience was so shallow (and I thought it so deep) that I am ashamed to say I immediately dismissed the book as 'eastern rubbish'. I didn't read it, but put it on a shelf somewhere, forgot about it and went on with my immature, noisy expression of what I believed to be the way.

Over the next ten years, I had begun experiencing a little more of the depth of God and had softened my resistance to meditation and expressions of faith other than the ones I knew. I even began investigating different paths to that great Mystery that we call God. One night I went looking for *Silent Music,* took it off the shelf, and didn't put it down until it was finished. About that same time, my friend, Barbara, gave me a copy of Thomas a Kempis' *'Of the Imitation of Christ'.* Those two books opened a door that began a hungry search for more of the same, and led me on a wonderful journey of discovery that will continue for the duration of my life.

The list below contains a few of the titles and authors that I found helpful on my journey to this point. Whilst every human journey is unique, I firmly believe that engaging with the mystery of God in ways other than only intellectual is essential for any of us to attain to any depth of spiritual experience and human maturity

Silent Music, William Johnson, Fontana, U.S.,1974

Of the imitation of Christ, Thomas a Kempis, Whittaker House, U.S., 1981

The Interior Castle, St Theresa of Avila, Halcyon Backhouse, U.K.,1988

Way of Perfection, St Theresa of Avila, Sheed and Ward, U.K. 1946

Experiencing the Depths of Jesus Christ, Jeanne Guyon, Seedsowers, U.S.

Revelations of Divine Love, Julian of Norwich, Penguin, U.K., 1966

The Cloud of Unknowing, unknown author, Penguin, U.K., 1961

Return to the Centre, Bede Griffiths, Fount, U.K., 1976

The Inner Christ, John Main,

The Selfless Self, Lawrence Freeman

Being in Love, William Johnson, Fount, U.K., 1988

The Still Point, William Johnson, Fordham, U.S., 1970

Lord, Teach us to Pray, William Johnson, Fount, U.K. 1990

Mystical Theology, William Johnson, Harper Collins, U.K., 1995

The Wounded Stag, William Johnson, Collins Fount, 1984

Mesiter Eckhart, Eds, Halcyon Backhouse, U.K., 1992

Awareness, Anthony de Mello, Doubleday, N.Y., 1990

Sadhana, Anthony de Mello, Harper Collins, U./K., 1978

Being Peace. Thich Nhat Hanh, Random House, U.K. 1987

The Miracle of Mindfulness, Thich Nhat Hanh, Rider, U.K., 1991

Saccidananda, Abhishiktananda (Dom Henri Le Saux) I.S.P.C.K., Delhi, 1974

The Further Shore, Abhishiktananda, I.S.P.C.K., Delhi

Lightning Source UK Ltd.
Milton Keynes UK
UKOW03f2115250316

270909UK00001B/127/P